W9-BWC-831

Uncle John's
BATHROOM READER
JINGLE BELL
CHRISTMAS

Uncle John's BATHROOM READER

JINGLE BELL CHRISTMAS

PORTABLE PRESS

Bathroom Readers' Institute
San Diego, California, and Ashland, Oregon

Uncle John's Bathroom Reader
Jingle Bell Christmas

Copyright © 2008 by Portable Press. All rights reserved.
No part of this book may be used or reproduced in any manner
whatsoever without written permission, except in the case of brief
quotations embodied in critical articles or reviews.

"Bathroom Reader," "Portable Press," and "Bathroom Readers'
Institute" are registered trademarks of Baker & Taylor, Inc.
All rights reserved.

For information, write The Bathroom Readers' Institute
Portable Press, 10350 Barnes Canyon Road, Suite 100,
San Diego, CA 92121
e-mail: unclejohn@btol.com

ISBN 13: 978-1-59223-914-6
ISBN 10: 1-59223-914-5

Library of Congress Cataloging-in-Publication Data

Uncle John's bathroom reader jingle bell Christmas.
    p. cm.
  ISBN 978-1-59223-914-6 (hardcover)
  1. Christmas. 2. Christmas—Humor. I. Title: Bathroom reader
jingle bell Christmas. II. Title: Jingle bell Christmas.
  GT4985.U544 2008
  394.2663—dc22

                                        2008017986

Printed in Canada
First printing: October 2008

08 09 10 11 12   10 9 8 7 6 5 4 3 2 1

Contents

Quote 'Em

As in Olden Days

Christmas on the Road

Wrap It Up

Here We Come a Caroling

Laughing All the Way

Santa's Grab Bag

Legends and Lore

Entertainment to Put You in the Holiday Spirit

*   *   *

Christmas Wish

"Backward, turn backward, / Oh Time, in your flight, / Make me a child again, just for tonight."

—*Elizabeth Akers Allen*

Thank You!

The Bathroom Readers' Institute sincerely thanks the following people whose hard work and assistance made this book possible.

Gordon Javna

JoAnn Padgett

Melinda Allman

Julia Papps

Jahnna Beecham

Malcolm Hillgartner

Michael Brunsfeld

Jeff Altemus

Angela Kern

Amy Miller

Duncan McCallum
and Friesens

Kait Fairchild

Thom Little

Brian Boone

Jay Newman

Dan Mansfield

Bonnie Vandewater

Sydney Stanley

Monica Maestas

Lisa Meyers

Amy Ly

Santa Claus, Mrs. Claus,
the reindeer, and the elves

"Jingle bells, jingle bells, jingle all the way . . ."

That's the first Christmas carol many of us learn as children. Just the sound of one little jingle bell can evoke visions of sleigh rides, reindeer, and Santa Claus.

This year at the Bathroom Readers' Institute, our stockings have been hung by the chimney with care and stuffed with hundreds of new weird and wonderful facts about Christmas. We found out who sent the first Christmas cards, and discovered that *Treasure Island* author Robert Louis Stevenson was a big softie when it came to the holidays. We know how astronauts celebrate Christmas in space and learned about some holiday hazards to avoid here on Earth. So if you're . . .

- Dreaming of a white Christmas, find out how to buy one on eBay.

- Planning to deck your halls with an artificial Christmas tree this year, learn about their evolution from goose feathers to toilet brushes to fiber optics.

- Hoping to hear real sleigh bells ring on Christmas, plan a visit to Belltown, USA, in Connecticut.

What we've discovered is that even as toys, cards, and decorations become increasingly high tech, the joy we find in Christmas remains simple and timeless. Even if today's tinsel isn't made of real silver like it was in the 19th century, it still drapes our Christmas trees, and children still write heartfelt letters to the North Pole. Volunteers ring bells by Salvation Army red kettles, and Secret Santas everywhere bring joy to others.

So from our family to yours, a merry Christmas to all, and to all a good read. And as always, go with the flow.

—Uncle John and the BRI Staff

Secret Santa

*Here's how one Secret Santa inspired
many to "pay it forward."*

A Simple Twist of Fate

During the winter of 1971, young Larry Stewart from
Mississippi was at the end of his rope. The college dropout
was out of work and out of money. He'd been sleeping in his
car for more than a week and hadn't eaten for two days when
he walked into the Dixie Diner and ordered a big meal.
When the bill came, he claimed to have lost his wallet. When
the owner walked over to the counter, Stewart braced for the
worst. To his amazement, though, the owner dropped a $20
bill in his hand and said, "You must've dropped this." The
drifter decided right then to honor that stranger's kindness
by helping other people in need whenever he could.

Mystery Man

Fast-forward to Christmas a decade later in Kansas City,
Missouri. Over the holidays, a mysterious stranger started
showing up in bus stations, thrift stores, laundromats, and
skid-row hotels, handing out $100 bills to people down on

their luck. With a hurried "Merry Christmas," the Secret Santa would walk away before the startled recipient of the gift could ask who he was.

The Beard Comes Off

This went on for 26 years, until finally in 2006, the Secret Santa was revealed to be Larry Stewart, now a successful businessman who'd made a fortune in telecommunications. He estimated that he'd given away more than $1.3 million over the years to needy people all over the United States. After 9/11, he went to New York and, in 2002, to Washington, D.C., shortly after the region was traumatized by sniper attacks. In 2003 he traveled to San Diego, California, to lend a helping hand after the city's wildfires.

Why had the legendary Secret Santa decided to reveal his identity? Stewart had been diagnosed with cancer and wanted to enlist new Santas to continue his work. He died in 2007, but others have picked up the tradition and carried on. Now every holiday season, Secret Santas fan out all over the United States, and like Larry Stewart, they hand out $100 bills to people in need . . . with the simple request that others pass on the kindness in whatever way they can.

* * *

First country with a Christmas postage stamp: Austria in 1937.

Christmas by the Numbers

Gifts, decorations, food, drink—it all really adds up.

25

Number of years a fruitcake can age and still be OK to eat. (Forty-seven percent of people say they'd toss a fruitcake in the trash if they got one as a gift.)

200

Number of mince pies Gus the camel ate after he broke out of his pen at an Irish riding school's 2006 Christmas party. (He also guzzled several cans of Guinness, which he opened with his teeth.)

221 feet

Tallest Christmas tree: a Douglas fir set up in Seattle's Northgate Shopping Center in 1950.

364

Number of presents you would receive if you got every gift mentioned in "The Twelve Days of Christmas."

500
Average number of fires caused by Christmas trees each year in the United States.

569
Average number of kids hospitalized annually for eating a Christmas ornament.

50,000
The number of letters the post office at Nuuk, Greenland, receives each year addressed to Santa Claus.

300,000 yards
The amount of ribbon and bows draped over 1,360 Christmas trees at Florida's Walt Disney World Resort each year.

30–35 million
Number of real Christmas trees sold in the United States every year. (Americans also buy 7 million artificial trees annually.)

300 million+
The number of homes Santa visits on Christmas Eve.

Jingle Bells Rock!

*Ring, ring, ring . . . here comes the history of
jingle bells. (The instrument and the song.)*

Sleigh Bells Ring . . .

Strings of bells tied to horses date back to the Roman
Empire. Then in medieval times, English knights hung single
bells of gold or silver, called *crotals*, on their horses as symbols of good luck. They believed that the bells would protect
the wearers from disease and harm because the noise would
scare off evil spirits.

Over the centuries, though, horse bells lost their supersti-
tious quality and became ornaments for wagons and sleighs.
They also took on a more practical role—as a way to let people know someone was coming, especially on dark, foggy, or
narrow roads. Sleighs, in particular, move quietly and can be
hard to stop quickly, so as the eastern United States and
Canada were settled, local governments started requiring that
bells be attached to sleighs. In fact, Canada's Ontario
province still has a law on its books that says "every person
traveling on a highway with a sleigh or sled drawn by a horse
or other animal shall have at least two bells attached to the

harness or to the sleigh or sled in such a manner as to give ample warning sound." (The penalty for no bells? $5.)

Belltown, USA

By the early 19th century, small businesses in New England had started manufacturing bells, but one town became known for them. In 1808 William Barton opened the first bell-making company in East Hampton, Connecticut. Two decades later, in 1832, a young man named William Bevin (who'd been an indentured servant of Barton's) and his brother Chauncey set up their own company: Bevin Bells. Before long, more bell businesses had moved in to East Hampton—30 in all. And by the early 1900s, the town produced 90 percent of the world's sleigh bells, earning it the nickname "Belltown, USA."

Only the Bevin brothers were able to survive the Great Depression, though, and today, the Bevin family still makes bells in East Hampton. They specialize in sleigh bells, and according to sixth generation owner Stanley Bevin, "We like to think that we've definitely contributed to the joy that Santa spreads."

And What About the Song?

"Jingle Bells" has become one of the most well-known Christmas carols in the world. It's been translated into almost every major language and was even the first song to be broadcast in space: in 1965, astronauts Tom Stafford and Wally Schirra serenaded Mission Control with a harmonica and sleigh-bell version of the song during the flight of *Gemini 6*.

But for all the song's popularity, its origin isn't as clear. In fact, there are two versions of how "Jingle Bells" came to be, though both attribute its creation to an amateur musician named James Pierpont.

Story #1: A native of Medford, Massachusetts, Pierpont was inspired to write a song called "One Horse Open Sleigh" (which later became "Jingle Bells") while watching a local sleigh race in 1850.

Story #2: In 1857 Pierpont was working as a choir director in Savannah, Georgia. He wrote the song for his church's Thanksgiving program, but it was so catchy and the kids loved it so much that they sang it again at the Christmas service.

Either way, Pierpont published the song in 1857, and the Library of Congress still has the original. "Jingle Bells" actually has four verses and a chorus that tell of a thrilling sleigh ride. The tune we all sing today is the first verse and the chorus.

*   *   *

First president to decorate an official tree: Franklin Pierce.

7

The Christmas Spider

According to a folk legend from Germany, this is how the tradition of draping Christmas trees with tinsel began. It is also why, on some trees, you might spy a jeweled spider tucked in among the ornaments.

Once upon a time, a German wife eagerly prepared her house for Christmas Eve. As she swept the house clean, all of the spiders were chased out of the rooms and upstairs into the attic. Then she decorated the Christmas tree with beautiful handmade ornaments and placed a present for each of her children under the tree.

The spiders that huddled in the attic were anxious to see the newly decorated tree and gifts. So, when the housewife went to bed, they crept down the stairs to peek at the tree. It was magnificent, and they couldn't resist climbing all over it, taking closer looks at each ornament and present. But as the clock began to toll midnight, the spiders realized that wherever they had crawled, they'd left a telltale mark—the entire tree was covered in spiderwebs. The spiders were afraid that the housewife would be furious when she saw what they had done and would kill them.

Then an angel appeared. It told the spiders not to fear and, touching the webs, turned them into beautiful strands of silver and gold. But, the angel said, the miracle came with a cost: one spider had to stay behind on the tree forever to remind us all of the "sacrifice of one for many."

* * *

America's Most Famous Christmas Tree

The Rockefeller Center Christmas tree in New York City has been delighting holiday lovers for years. Here are some of its most important dates:

- **1931:** Workmen building the plaza erected a small tree to celebrate receiving their Christmas paychecks—a big deal during the Great Depression.

- **1933:** The first formal tree went up, covered with 700 lights.

- **1942:** Three trees were set up. Because of World War II blackouts, there were no lights this year, but each tree was decorated in a patriotic color: one in red, one white, and one blue.

- **1964:** The tree lighting ceremony had become an annual event. It was first broadcast locally in 1951, but it wasn't until the 1960s that enough American homes had television sets to make the broadcast a nationwide event.

Christmas Customs

*Along with lighting a Yule log, trimming a tree, and decking
the halls, in many cultures, Christmas is also a time
to prepare for and predict the future.*

- After Christmas Eve dinner, unmarried Polish girls place a piece of fish on the floor and let a dog into the room. The girl whose fish the dog eats first is the next to get married.

- During Christmas dinner, Lithuanians and Poles examine their shadows cast on the wall by the candlelight. A large, wide, and complete shadow indicates the New Year will go well. A thin, wavering, or indistinct shadow foretells a difficult year. If the shadow is missing a head, watch out. That means catastrophe is a certainty.

- On Christmas Eve, Scandinavians place their shoes side by side. This assures harmony in the home for the next year.

- To ward off misfortune in the new year, Greeks burn all their old shoes.

- During the Christmas holidays, the Scots pour ale into the ocean to ensure a profitable year of fishing.

- In Germany it's customary to eat lots of greasy pancakes

on the winter solstice, and to leave a few for Frau Holda, the fairy who shakes out her down cape to reveal a flock of white geese; their feathers cover crops to protect them from early or late frosts.

- After the Christmas dinner, Czechs sail walnut boats (shells with tiny lit candles in them) in a large bowl of water. If your boat navigates the bowl safely, relax—your New Year will be blessed with prosperity. But bad luck awaits those whose boats sink to the bottom.

*   *   *

A Superstitious Season

- Lithuanians believe the moment the clock strikes midnight on Christmas Eve, all animals are able to speak like humans. They chatter on about many things, but be forewarned: it's never a good idea to listen to them—you might learn the day of your death.

- The Irish believe that Christmas Eve is an excellent night on which to die, since it is the night the gates of heaven are open to everyone.

- Swedes believe that dangerous trolls roam the countryside from dusk on Christmas Eve until dawn on Christmas morning, so it's best to stay inside.

Season's Greetings

The tradition of sending Christmas cards began in Victorian England with a man who had more money than time.

I n the 1800s, English schoolchildren often gave their parents gifts of handwritten Christmas letters, carefully printed on decorated paper. People in Europe and America, particularly businessmen, gave New Year's notes to their best clients. But it wasn't until 1843, when Sir Henry Cole of London decided to have his Christmas greetings printed, that the world saw the first official Christmas card.

Only a Shilling

Cole was the first director of London's Victoria and Albert Museum of Art and Design; he also ran an art store on Baker Street. When he found himself short on time and wanting to send Christmas greetings to all of his friends, he commissioned artist John Callcott Horsely to design a card with a seasonal image and an appropriate message.

Horsely came up with a triptych that included three generations of a happy English family toasting the season with cups of wine. On the surrounding panels were images of ordinary people doing good deeds for the poor. Horsely wanted to remind his wealthy client of the poverty that afflicted so many people in England at the time. (The card also provoked an outcry from temperance groups for being "politically incorrect" because the children in the family shown on the card were drinking wine right along with their elders.) The printed message read, "A Merry Christmas and a Happy New Year to You." Cole ordered 1,000 of the cards, sent them to his friends, and sold the leftovers for a shilling each.

The Penny Black

The Christmas that Cole mailed his cards was also the Christmas that steam-powered presses had drastically reduced the costs of printing colored cards. And the 1840 introduction of Great Britain's first postage stamp—the "penny black"—had made it cheaper and faster to mail cards than to deliver them by hand or messenger. In 1880 the British Post Office first advised patrons to "Post early for Christmas." All of these things came together and opened the door for card publishers like Charles Goodall & Son, one of the first companies to mass-produce Christmas and visiting cards. The company became known for its border designs of holly, mistletoe, and robins. And Kate Greenaway, Walter Crane, and Thomas Crane were among the 19th-century artists famous for their card designs.

The Trick Card

The most popular Christmas cards of the Victorian era were trick cards. These had a wide variety of artistic designs, but always featured a surprise. With the turn of a page, with the pull of a string, or by the move of a lever, a new card part would be revealed. One typical card had yellow, red, and white roses in a fan-shaped handle. The reader pulled a silk thread dangling from the handle, and the card opened to twice its size, revealing five rose petals imprinted with quotes from William Wordsworth and John Keats. And one racy Christmas card revealed a woman's dancing legs.

For a while, it was popular to have trick cards include reproductions of money and checks. These were so realistic that recipients often tried to spend the money. The cards had themes like the "Bank of Love," the "Bank of Blessings," and "Ten Thousand Joys." Other trick cards had reproductions of train tickets with destinations like "Prosperity" and "Happiness" printed on the tickets. The trick cards were so popular that Victorians kept scrapbooks of them and shared them with friends throughout the year.

For more about Christmas cards,
turn to page 49.

Toy Wars

*Over the years, parents have proven they're willing to fight
to get the hottest present for their darlings.*

Cabbage Patch Kids (1982)

These stuffed dolls with faces only a mother could love sup-
posedly came from BabyLand General Hospital and included
adoption agreements. Sales reached an all-time high in 1985
at $600 million.

Christmas chaos: Crazed shoppers eager to adopt one of
these babies trampled a pregnant woman and a 75-year-old
man at two different stores. An employee at a Zayres store in
Wilkes-Barre, Pennsylvania, used a baseball bat to fend off
the Cabbage Patch kooks, but one customer still suffered a
broken leg in the stampede.

Tickle Me Elmo (1996)

Tickle Me Elmo, the furry red monster doll from *Sesame
Street*, giggled his way to a million units sold during
Christmas of 1996.

Christmas chaos: A Wal-Mart employee in New Brunswick,
Canada, was placing one of the dolls on the shelf when he

was run over by a mob of 300 people battling to bag one of 49 remaining Elmos. Hence the nickname the doll got in the press: "Trample Me Elmo."

Furby (1998)

These funny, talking gizmos set the fur flying in stores around the country.

Christmas chaos: Customers who had braved the cold all night in Lynn, Massachusetts, started a riot when they discovered that Wal-Mart had stocked only 30 of the little electronic gremlins. Furby shoppers in Denver knocked over displays and trampled bystanders. And in Illinois, two women were injured in another Furby stampede. Frantic parents then turned to eBay, where they paid three times the sticker price.

PlayStation 3 (2006)

When they were first introduced, these $500 game boxes went for as high as $3,300 on eBay.

Christmas chaos: Consumers who didn't want to be gouged online threw themselves into the fray on the streets, prompting gaming critics to quip, "violent games beget violent actions." Armed robbers in California made off with four PlayStations. And four shoppers who camped outside a Best Buy in Lexington, Kentucky, were shot by a lunatic toting a BB gun.

Now, That's Just Nuts!

- When the assistant manager of the Bend, Wisconsin, Wal-Mart went to open the store, he found 50 customers waiting outside in the cold, determined to buy a PlayStation. Unfortunately, the store had only 10 in stock. Faced with a potential riot, the assistant manager made a hasty decision—he told the customers they could compete for the PlayStations in an impromptu game of musical chairs. He set 10 chairs in a line outside the store. On the shout of "Go!" the shoppers stampeded toward the line, shoving, kicking, and diving headfirst into the chairs. One man fell and bruised his head and knee. Another hit his head on a lamppost and had to be taken to the hospital in an ambulance.

- Two disc jockeys in Milwaukee, Wisconsin, joked that a load of 2,000 Cabbage Patch Kids would be dropped from a B-29 bomber to people who held up catcher's mitts and American Express cards at County Stadium. Two dozen hopefuls actually showed up with mitts and cards in hand.

*   *   *

I will honor Christmas in my heart, and try to keep it all the year.

—Charles Dickens

Christmas Party Games: Victorian Style

Looking for something different to do at your next holiday party? Consider these games, which were popular with Victorian England's upper class.

The Minister's Cat

Supplies: A healthy knowledge of adjectives and the ability to clap a rhythm in unison

How to play: Everyone gathers around in a circle, and each player comes up with an adjective to describe the minister's cat, beginning with the letter A. (Don't tell anyone your adjective.) The game begins with all the participants clapping in rhythm, such as clapping their thighs twice, followed by clapping their hands twice. While still clapping, the first person describes the minister's cat. For example, "The minister's cat is an ANGELIC cat." Then each player takes a turn until everyone has had a chance to describe the minister's cat with the letter A. Subsequent rounds begin with the next letter in the alphabet. Anyone who states a word that repeats or does not begin with the correct letter or who is stumped is out.

Shadows (or Shadow Buff)

Supplies: A small table, a lamp or candle, a stool, and a large white tablecloth or sheet

How to play: This game requires that players not only guess whose shadow has been thrown, but also to come up with ingenious ways to disguise their own shadows. Suspend the sheet along one side of the room. Place the table with the light behind the sheet, allowing ample room for participants to walk between the sheet and the table. Center the stool on the other side of the sheet (where the player who is "it" will sit) while everyone else lines up behind the sheet. Turn off all the lights except for the candle or lamp. One by one, each player parades in front of the light, casting a shadow on the sheet. The person sitting on the stool must guess whose shad-

ow is whose. Shadow-casters have the freedom to alter their shadows: they can hunch their backs, duckwalk, or even use their clothing to change their shape. Anything goes, as long as it's not an added object. (You can't use a carrot to make your nose look bigger, for instance.) Play continues until the person who is it correctly identifies one of the shadow-casters.

The Picture Frame

Supplies: An empty picture frame

How to play: Each player takes a turn at being the "picture" by holding the frame in front of his or her face and remaining still for one minute. The task for the challengers is to cause the "picture" to lose composure. Challengers can pull faces, make odd sounds, tell jokes, or stand on their heads if they want to, but they are not allowed to touch the player holding the frame—so no tickling allowed!

Yawning for Cheshire Cheese

Supplies: A block of Cheshire cheese and a horde of tired guests

How to play: This game should come at the end of the evening. It requires simply that guests sit in a circle and yawn at one another. Whoever produces the longest, biggest, loudest yawn wins the block of Cheshire cheese.

*   *   *

A little ice is always nice. More diamonds are sold at Christmas than at any other time of year.

Treats of Yore

*What might you have found in your Christmas
stocking in the olden days?*

Sugarplums

They dance in our heads in "The Night Before Christmas,"
and one even became a fairy in *The Nutcracker Suite*. But
what exactly is a sugarplum? In the 1600s, sugarplums were a
comfit, a sugarcoated seed, but by Victorian times, they were
mostly made of currants and raisins (which were called plums
back then) boiled in sugar many times to create a hard candy.
Eventually, recipes didn't call for any fruit at all, just hard-
boiled sugar.

Oranges

Children in the 19th and early 20th centuries were excited to
get an exotic orange for Christmas. It was a tasty treat that
usually only the rich could enjoy because all citrus fruits had
to be shipped from faraway places. Even today, many children find an orange tucked in the toes of their stockings, a
holdover from their parents' or grandparents' generations.

Gingerbread

Gingerbread appeared in Europe at the end of the 11th century shortly after returning Crusaders brought ginger roots back from the Middle East. Bakers realized that adding ginger didn't just make cakes and breads taste better—it helped preserve them, too. So ginger quickly became a kitchen staple. Because gingerbread was pliable (about the consistency of Play-Doh), bakers started forming it into wooden molds, cutting it into decorative shapes (hearts were especially popular), and decorating it with sugar. But by the 1400s, gingerbread baking was considered such a refined skill that it was placed under the complete control of the baking guilds. No one was allowed to bake gingerbread at home.

In 1643 the baker's guild in Nuremburg, Germany, took gingerbread (or *lebkuchen*) to a new level. Master bakers created elaborate gingerbread works of art decorated with frosting and gold leaf. The creations of the *lebkucheners*, as the Nuremburg bakers called themselves, were so prized that they were used like currency to pay taxes and purchase goods. And Nuremberg became known as the "Gingerbread Capital of the World"—a title it still holds today.

To read about some amazing gingerbread creations, turn to page 108.

The Alphabet Carol Quiz

It's as easy as ABC. (Answers on page 175.)

U ncle John feels lucky when he can remember more than the first line of a Christmas carol, let alone the whole song. Imagine his joy when he came upon this Alphabet Carol Quiz. Each capital letter is the first letter of a word in the opening line of a familiar Christmas carol. You don't have to know anything beyond the opening line and the title of the carol. For instance: JBJBJATW = "Jingle Bells" (Jingle bells, jingle bells, jingle all the way . . .). Read the clue and hint, figure out the first line, identify the song—and you're a winner!

1. IDOAWC (Hint: Fifth word, "white.")

2. AIAMNCFAB (Hint: Sixth word, "crib.")

3. OTWOIF (Hint: Third word, "weather.")

4. JTTWTLIC (Hint: Last word, "come.")

5. OTFDOCMTLGTM (Hint: Ninth word, "love.")

6. ISMKSC (Hint: Third word, "Mommy.")

7. YBWOYBNC (Hint: First word, "You.")

8. TFNTADS (Hint: Fifth word, "angels.")

9. SNHN (Hint: Third word, "holy.")

10. FTSWAJHS (Hint: Sixth word, "jolly.")

11. WTKOOA (Hint: Second word, "three.")

12. SBRAYL (Hint: First word, "Sleigh.")

13. ICUTMC (Hint: Third word, "upon.")

14. CROAOF (Sixth word, "fire.")

*   *   *

Dear Pére Noel . . .

After being told by the local government that there wasn't
enough money in the budget to replace their broken patrol
cars, the police of Marignane, France, drafted this letter to
"Pére Noel" to ask for help:

> Dear Santa,
>
> Our cars can't handle the job any more. If you think
> we are exaggerating, you can try out the cars your
> self. Even your sleigh is better than one of them.
>
> Santa listened—the cops got new cars.

Christmas in the
White House

Ever wonder how the president's kids spend the holidays?

Susannah Adams, 1801

John Adams was the first president to live at 1600
Pennsylvania Avenue in Washington, D.C. He was also the
first president to hold a children's party—for his four-year-
old granddaughter, Susannah. During the party in 1801, a
child broke a toy dish belonging to Susannah, who took
revenge by biting off the nose of a new wax doll intended for
her guest.

Tad Lincoln, 1863

While they were living in the White House, President
Abraham Lincoln's 10-year-old son Tad befriended a turkey
given as a gift to the family. Tad named the turkey Jack and
led him on walks around the White House grounds. As
December 25 neared and it became apparent that Jack was
going to be Christmas dinner, Tad burst into a cabinet meet-
ing and pleaded with his father to spare Jack's life. He made

such a good case that President Lincoln wrote a formal
pardon for the turkey.

Archie and Quentin Roosevelt, 1902

President Theodore Roosevelt banned Christmas trees from
the White House out of concern for the conservation of
forests. But his sons (eight-year-old Archie and five-year-old
Quentin) ignored the ban. They sneaked a tree up the back
stairs of the White House and hid it in a closet. (These boys
were especially good at sneaking—they once even sneaked
their pony, Algonquin, up the elevator into Archie's room.)

On Christmas morning, the boys
threw open the closet, revealing
a tree filled with presents for
each family member.

President Roosevelt was
impressed but decided
the boys needed a
talking-to. So he
sent them to
Gifford
Pinchot, head
of the
National
Forest
Service, to learn
about conservation.

To Roosevelt's surprise, Pinchot explained that fire, not cutting Christmas trees, posed the worst threat to America's national forests. He even said that if done right, cutting some trees is a good idea because it thins out a forest and allows smaller trees to grow. Also, Pinchot said Christmas tree farms were a good way for farmers to use otherwise untillable land. (No word on whether or not Teddy Roosevelt's family had Christmas trees after that.)

Caroline Kennedy, 1962

President John F. Kennedy's five-year-old daughter Caroline wrote this letter to Santa:

Dear Santa,

I would like a pair of silver skates—and one of those horse wagons with lucky dips—and Susie Smart and Candy Fashion dolls and a real pet reindeer and a clock to tell time and a covered wagon and a farm and you decide anything else. And interesting planes or a bumpy thing he can ride in or some noisy thing or something he can push or pull for John [Jr.].

Love, from Caroline

*   *   *

Sweet! More than 1.76 billion candy canes are sold every Christmas.

I Get a Kick Out of You

For more than 75 years, the Rockettes have performed four shows a day, 28 shows a week, during the Christmas season.

Meet Them in St. Louis

In the beginning, there was Russell Markert's high-kicking, tap-dancing Missouri Rockets. Markert had seen a group of women perform a kick line in *The Ziegfeld Follies* of 1922 and got the idea to hire his own dancers to do the same thing . . . only better. His dancers would be taller, with longer legs, and thus able to kick higher than anyone had before. He choreographed intricate routines designed to make the women appear to move as "one dancer." Each person in the line looked and moved just like the others—down to the steps, costumes, hair, and makeup. And putting the tallest dancers in the center and gradually decreasing the height, with the shortest women at either end, created the illusion of uniform height. The Missouri Rockets made their debut in 1925 in St. Louis and were an instant hit.

Roxyettes

S. L. "Roxy" Rothafel, a showman from New York, caught

one of the Missouri Rockets' shows and was impressed, so he brought them to the Big Apple to perform at his theater, the Roxy. Rothafel put his own imprint on the group by renaming them the "Roxyettes." They performed at the Roxy with a variety of famous acts, including the Flying Wallendas high-wire troupe, Ray Bolger (who played the Scarecrow in *The Wizard of Oz*), and modern dance legend Martha Graham. But it was the 16 Roxyettes' eye-high kicks and precision dance movements that really wowed New York audiences.

Rockettes

On December 27, 1932, the Roxyettes opened at Radio City Music Hall under a brand-new name, the Rockettes. The troupe had doubled in size to a company of 36 women who presented a new show each week. The next year, Radio City introduced "The Radio City Christmas Spectacular," and ever since, the Rockettes have been singing and kicking their way into the hearts of millions.

Russell Markert, founder, director, and choreographer, stayed with the company through all the changes and staged the routines until he retired in 1971.

The Numbers
2½ inches

Height of the heels the Rockettes wear during performances.

5 feet, 6 inches to 5 feet, 10½ inches

The height range of a Rockette dancer.

8

Number of complete costume changes, including hats and shoes, that each Rockette makes during the show.

10 minutes

Time it takes Claudia Diaz, the Rockettes' fastest seamstress, to replace a zipper.

25

Number of assistants who help the Rockettes make their costume changes.

200

Number of high kicks the Rockettes perform during every show.

1,400

Number of dance tights used in a single season.

To read more about the show,
turn to page 135.

Five Christmas Films (You May Not Have Heard Of)

Tired of the annual dose of It's a Wonderful Life *and* Miracle on 34th Street*? Here are some overlooked holiday gems.*

Babes in Toyland (1934)

Legendary comedians Laurel and Hardy star as a couple of bumbling toymakers who get into trouble at work . . . with hilarious results. Set in a Mother Goose fantasy world (there's even a subplot of a Scrooge-like villain trying to throw the Old Lady Who Lived in a Shoe out of her . . . um . . . shoe), the film features lavish production numbers and some endearing overacting. But front and center are the antics of one of the greatest comedy teams of all time. (There have been several *Babes in Toyland* remakes, but the Laurel and Hardy version is a classic.)

Remember the Night (1940)

Four years before they appeared together onscreen in the film noir thriller *Double Indemnity*, Barbara Stanwyck and Fred MacMurray starred in this holiday comedy scripted by

Preston Sturges. A no-nonsense Manhattan district attorney (MacMurray) has a moment of pity (it's almost Christmas) and posts bail for an accused shoplifter (Stanwyck), only to find her on his doorstep with no place to go. So he takes her to his mother's farm in Indiana. The two antagonists fall in love, which makes for an awkward tangle when they return to New York for her trial.

Beyond Tomorrow (1940)

A warmhearted twist on the Three Wise Men story: the ghosts of three old codgers (C. Aubrey Smith, Harry Carey, and Charles Winninger) watch over a pair of young sweethearts as they meet on a fateful Christmas Eve, fall in love, and weather the inevitable bumpy ride down the rocky road to love. Along with marvelous performances from the three old hams, Maria Ouspenskaya (twice nominated for an Oscar) nearly steals the show as their Russian servant.

Christmas in Connecticut (1945)

Barbara Stanwyck plays a Martha Stewart–like columnist who's famous the world over as a paragon of domesticity— except that she's a fake. She writes columns about an imaginary family and charming home in Connecticut from her Manhattan penthouse. A wounded sailor's wish to have dinner with the columnist throws her life into a tizzy, as she tries to maintain the story at a borrowed house in Connecticut over the Christmas holiday. The whole thing is further complicated by the fact that she falls for the sailor (Dennis Morgan).

Come to the Stable (1949)

A pair of charming French nuns (Loretta Young and Celeste Holm) come to Bethlehem, Connecticut, to build a children's hospital. With the help of a collection of quirky locals, they make their hospital a reality. Based on a story by Clare Boothe Luce, this film received seven Oscar nominations and featured some of Hollywood's best-loved character actors, like Dooley Wilson (Sam in *Casablanca*).

For more movies, turn to page 88.

*   *   *

And Now, Something Uplifting

If you happen to have $12.5 million lying around, consider purchasing one of Victoria's Secret's Fantasy Bras. The 2005 Fantasy Bra was loaded with 2,900 diamonds, rubies, and other precious stones. If that's too pricey, consider the 2007 version, which even came with accessories like a matching bracelet and barrette. That one went for a mere $4 million.

Carols by Candlelight

*We all celebrate Christmas a little differently. Here's one
Australian tradition that unites that country in song.*

An Inspirational Walk

On Christmas Eve in 1937, Australian radio announcer
Norman Banks was walking home after work when he
noticed an elderly woman sitting by a window. Her face was
lit by the glow of a single candle, and she was singing "Away
in a Manger" along with her radio. Banks wondered how
many other people were sitting alone on Christmas Eve with
only the radio as company. The vision inspired Banks to
create a gathering where people could come together to sing
carols by candlelight.

At midnight the following Christmas Eve, at the Alexandra
Gardens in Melbourne, a choir of 30 singers, two soloists, the
Metropolitan Fire Brigade Band, and 10,000 carolers assem-
bled to celebrate Christmas by singing carols together. The
only light came from the stars above and the candles everyone held. The evening was such a big hit that on Christmas
Eve the next year, almost 40,000 people attended.

Sing a Song of Christmas

Now, every weekend in the month of December there is a "Carols by Candlelight" celebration happening somewhere in Australia. Towns often print song lyrics in the newspaper, and locals meet in the park carrying blankets, a picnic dinner, and a candle. At dusk, the carolers light their candles and the singing begins.

On Christmas Eve, "Carols by Candlelight" is broadcast live from the Sydney Myer Music Bowl in Melbourne, with all proceeds going to Vision Australia, an organization that helps the blind and vision-impaired. In 2007 the event raised more than $800,000.

*　　*　　*

Christmas Present of the Future

According to inventor Ray M. Alden of Raleigh, North Carolina, invisibility is just a matter of becoming chameleon-like. So in 2003, he designed a process that weaves photodetectors and light emitters into fabric. The cloak maps your immediate environment, and the light emitters adjust the coloring of the cloak to match. Voilà . . . invisibility! (Subsequent research by scientist David R. Smith of Duke University and John Pendry of the University of London resulted in the 2006 announcement of an actual working prototype.)

Holiday Greetings from Heaven

Chet Fitch of Ashland, Oregon, died in October 2007. Two months later, 34 of his friends received Christmas cards from him . . . with "Heaven" listed as the return address.

The Best-Laid Plans

Twenty years earlier, Fitch, a well-known practical joker, had started making plans for what he figured would be his final prank. He enlisted the help of his barber, Patty Dean, to help him pull it off. Fitch printed cards featuring a photo of him and his wife Jessie indulging in their favorite pastime, square danc-ing. He wrote a final Christmas message to his friends, addressed the envelopes, and gave them to Dean, with instructions to mail them the Christmas after he died.

Patient Prankster

Years passed, and Fitch kept in touch with Patty Dean, sending more money for postage when rates increased and passing on his friends' changes of address. Fitch's wife died in 1995, and finally, in 2007, the 88-year-old Fitch stopped into the barbershop to visit Dean. "You must be getting tired of waiting to mail those cards," he told her. "I think you'll probably be able to mail them this year." Fitch died two weeks later.

Last Call

Patty Dean kept her promise to her fun-loving friend and dutifully mailed the Christmas cards. Here's what Chet Fitch wrote:

> I asked Big Guy if I could sneak back and send some cards. At first he said no; but at my insistence he finally said, "Oh well, what the heaven, go ahead but don't tarry there." Wish I could tell you about things here but words cannot explain. Better get back as Big Guy said he stretched a point to let me in the first time, so I had better not press my luck. I'll probably be seeing you (some sooner than you think).

> Wishing you a very Merry Christmas. Chet Fitch

*   *   *

Last state to make Christmas a holiday: Oklahoma in 1907.

Sing a Song of Christmas

Did you know that many of our favorite
Christmas carols began as hymns?

Hymnals in the 18th century were usually published as books of poetry. For the most part, there was no music printed in them, only the words. So any hymn could be set to any tune that fit the verses' meter. Here are three hymns that got new tunes and words and become Christmas classics.

"Joy to the World"

Isaac Watts wrote more that 600 hymns, but arguably his most famous was "Joy to the World," which he penned in 1719. It wasn't until about 1839 that American composer Lowell Mason set it to the tune we know today—a tune many scholars think Mason pinched from German composer George Frideric Handel, of *Messiah* fame.

"What Child Is This?"

The song "Greensleeves" was written in 1580 by Richard Jones (although it is believed that King Henry VIII, an accomplished composer and musician, was the author). By the 18th century, there were at least four different songs set to the "Greensleeves" tune. In 1865 William Chatterton Dix set three stanzas of his poem "The Manger Throne" to the familiar tune, and the more commonly known Christmas carol "What Child Is This?" was born.

"Hark! The Herald Angels Sing"

When Charles Wesley showed his brother John Wesley, the great Methodist evangelist, and friend George Whitfield his new hymn, they balked at the first line. "Hark! How all the welkin rings!" sounded too old-fashioned. (It was, after all, 1739, and "welkin," meaning "sky or firmament," was a medieval word.) So Whitfield changed the line to "Hark! The herald angels sing." Then in 1855 English musician W. H. Cummings matched

parts of Felix Mendelssohn's 1840 cantata melody with the words from Wesley's hymn, creating the Christmas carol we sing today.

The Day the Sun Stands Still

Many people still celebrate one of the world's oldest Christmastime holidays: the winter solstice.

The word *solstice* is Latin for "sun stands still," and to ancient civilizations, the sun did appear to move very little during the solstice. (Today, we know it just looks that way because of how the earth is rotating.) The phenomenon occurs twice a year—in June and December. The summer solstice is on or near June 21, the longest day of the year; the winter solstice always takes place on or near December 21 and is the shortest day of the year. With the winter solstice, ancient people knew the days would start to be longer, and a new growing season was on the way.

An Ancient Observatory

The desire to predict exactly when the winter solstice would occur led to some of prehistory's most remarkable monuments. Maeshowe on the Orkney Islands off of northern Scotland and the Gavrinis tomb in Brittany, France, are two that date from around 3200 BC. But perhaps the greatest is the megalithic passage tomb (a type of burial site that's accessible by a long passageway) at Newgrange, Ireland.

This masterpiece of human engineering was built 1,000 years before Stonehenge and 500 years before the Egyptian pyramids. The early Irish who created it used only primitive stone tools, but had keen powers of observation. Newgrange is a mound of 200,000 tons of crushed rock that covers a 60-foot-long passage leading to a domed sanctuary. At daybreak on the winter solstice, a shaft of light enters the tomb through a narrow slit above the entrance. The sunbeam travels about 60 feet into the chamber, and for 17 minutes illuminates a stone basin inside.

From Osiris to Christmas

The Europeans weren't the only ones who celebrated the winter solstice. To welcome the "rebirth" of sunlight after the dark winter, cultures around the world held their own rituals and festivals:

- The ancient Egyptians celebrated the symbolic death and rebirth of Osiris by burying an effigy of the god in the inner shrine of a temple. At the winter solstice, priests emerged from the temple, carrying the image of a baby and proclaiming the god's rebirth with the new light.

- The most important festival for the Incas of South America was Inti Raymi, a winter solstice ritual that symbolized the eternal marriage of the sun god Wiracocha and human beings. It began with three days of fasting and ended with a nine-day celebration that included dancing and feasting. Francisco Pizarro's conquistadores tried to eradicate the practice when they conquered Peru in the 1500s, but it survived intact. Today, it's one of the largest annual festivals in South America.

- The Roman feast of Saturnalia honored the god Saturn and included a winter solstice celebration. The Romans called the winter solstice *natalis solis invicti*, the "birthday of the unconquered sun," and it prompted a weeklong festival devoted to merrymaking and feasting. During Saturnalia, schools closed, soldiers went on leave, and no criminals were executed. Neighbors went from house to house bringing gifts. Temples were draped with evergreen boughs and garlands, and masked revelers partied in the streets. Slaves were given the temporary freedom to do and say what they liked, and townspeople appointed a mock king to "rule" over the festivities. (This practice persisted into the Middle Ages, with Lords of Misrule being elected to preside over holiday celebrations in medieval manors and palaces.)

- Christianity didn't begin its own winter celebration until the Fourth century. Up until that time, Easter was the preeminent Christian festival, and there was little interest in celebrating the birth of Christ. (Only pagan gods had birthdays.) But by 350, Christian leaders had decided to celebrate Jesus's birth around the winter solstice, and they converted the old pagan festivities into Christian ones. As Christianity expanded into Europe, the new holiday fit perfectly with the ancient Norse and Germanic Yule celebrations. Move over, Saturnalia—hello, Christmas!

*   *   *

An Unlikely Santa

In 1862 the United States was in the midst of the seemingly endless Civil War. The conflict hadn't had the expected quick resolution, and tensions were strained among soldiers and civilians on both sides. But in Winchester, Virginia, a town the Union Army controlled, five young Confederate girls decided to confront a Union officer and ask for his help in buying Christmas presents for their teacher.

The occupying Union soldiers had forbidden all merchants from selling any supplies to the locals because they worried the goods would go to Confederate troops. So the girls, who attended a local school, took the $3 their class had raised and asked one of the Union colonels for permission to buy their teacher some coffee, sugar, and tea.

In the spirit of Christmas, the colonel was generous: he gave the girls "twenty pounds of sugar and a large packet of coffee and tea," much more than they could have bought.

Surprise Christmas Guest

*We thought this one was a hoax, but after some serious
investigation, we discovered it's 100 percent true.
Merry Christmas, from Spain.*

In Catalonia, Spain, a region along the country's border
with France, it's tradition to display a Nativity scene at
Christmas. And like most Nativity scenes around the world,
the ones in Catalonia include figurines of the standard
Christmas story characters: Jesus, Mary, Joseph, the Three
Wise Men, some shepherds, and a few sheep and cows. But
unlike other Nativity scenes, those in Catalonia feature one
more character—*El Caganer*.

El Who?

El Caganer is a shepherd with his pants around his ankles,
pooping. He shows up year-round and is usually found
squatting behind a bush or bale of hay, wearing the traditional
red Catalan hat and smoking a pipe. Ever since the late 17th
century, though, the region's Christmas Nativity scenes have
always included El Caganer, which translated literally means
"the great defecator."

Human Fertilizer

It's unclear exactly how the tradition started. But the Catalan people have always been a mostly agricultural society, and defecation was a symbol of fertility and a good crop. So the most commonly heard explanation is that El Caganer is there to fertilize the soil and bring forth a good harvest. He's also thought to bring good luck and prosperity to people who "invite" him into their homes.

Originally made of clay, today's El Caganer is usually made of plastic, and he comes in a variety of characters. Catalans no longer have to pick between a shepherd and a monk (the other traditional El Caganer). The modern pooping man can be a famous soccer player, police officer, actor, or rock star. There are even statues made of Santa Claus and political figures like President Nicolas Sarkozy of France and U.S. President George W. Bush.

And Speaking of Poop . . .

The region's children have their own special Yule log called the *caga tio*, or "pooping log." For two weeks before Christmas, the caga tio—a loaf-sized wooden log that has a face painted on it and that wears a red hat—sits on a table in the family's home. Every day, children and adults "feed" it (give it an offering of food or wine) until Christmas Day, when they move it to the hearth. Then, the children cover the caga tio with a blanket and hide while their parents put wrapped presents, candies, and treats under the cloth. Finally, the local kids beat the log with a stick while pulling out treats and chanting this song (translated for your convenience):

> *Poop log! Poop log!*
> *Poop candy for Christmas!*
> *If you don't, we'll whack you again!*

* * *

Dreaming of a White Christmas

Since 2006 the SNO! Zone Company of Great Britain has auctioned off a White Christmas on eBay. SNO! Zone, which operates three indoor ski slopes, promised to deliver a "personal winter wonderland" of snow in a refrigerated truck to the highest bidder. The deal included a "trained staff" who would not only arrange the snow but also string lights, provide a decorated tree for the house, and hang a wreath on the door. In 2007 SNO! Zone added caroling singers and a real Santa with a sack of presents.

In 2007 Chris Hopkins, manager of a catering company in Leeds, England, bid $2,800 for this White Christmas. But he didn't want it for himself or his company. It was a gift for the terminally ill kids at Martin House Hospice. "Christmas is for children," said Hopkins, "and bringing a smile to their faces made it worth every penny."

A Superstitious
Southern Christmas

*Every region has its own quirky holiday traditions.
These come from the Deep South.*

- If you fix your roof between Christmas and New Year's
  Day, the holes will come right back.

- If you wash and iron a Christmas present of clothes
  before giving it, you'll wash out the good luck and iron
  in the bad.

- Make sure to eat an apple just as the clock strikes twelve
  on Christmas Eve. That'll guarantee good health to you in
  the coming year.

- Wear something new on Christmas Day and your luck
  will change for the better. (Unless you decide to wear new
  shoes. Those will probably hurt and may even "walk you
  into a catastrophe," as the Southerners say.)

- Leave a loaf of bread on the table after Christmas Eve
  dinner and you'll have all the bread you need until the
  next Christmas.

- Don't let the fire go out on Christmas morning. If you do, spirits will haunt you.

- At midnight on Christmas Eve, barn animals drop to their knees, face Bethlehem . . . and talk about the meaning of Christmas. But if they catch you watching, you'll die.

*　　*　　*

Ten Unforgettable Christmas Songs (That You May Want to Forget)

1. "Mama's Twisting with Santa"—Mark Anthony and the Elves

2. "Ringo Bells"—Three Blonde Mice

3. "Here Comes Peter Cotton Claus"—Alex Houston and Elmer

4. "CB Santa"—Big Jim and the Goodbuddies

5. "Santa Got a DWI"—Sherwin Linton

6. "Jingle-O the Elf"—Tennessee Ernie Ford

7. "Christmas in My Pants"—Bob Rich

8. "Boogaloo Round the Aluminum Christmas Tree"—Carolee Goodgold

9. "I Want an Elf for Christmas"—Fountains of Wayne

10. "Dominick the Donkey (The Italian Christmas Donkey)"—Lou Monte

Father of the American Christmas Card

On page 12, we began the history of Christmas cards. It took 30 years for those decorated notes to make the leap from England to Germany . . . and then, finally, to America. Here's the rest of the story.

Gotta Get a Prang

Louis Prang, a German immigrant who set up a printing company in Boston, started selling Christmas cards in 1875. Prang's cards featured colorful floral arrangements of roses, daisies, gardenias, geraniums, and apple blossoms. Within six years, he was selling more than 5 million cards every year—equal to 10 percent of the U.S. population at the time.

Other American printers started making cards too, but the high quality of Prang's—he developed a technique to print multiple colors that made his designs stand out—brought him total dominance of the American market, earning him the title "Father of the American Christmas Card."

Money Business

Prang spared no expense in trying to create the most unique

cards on the market. He commissioned the best artists of his era—including people like Winslow Homer, famous for his landscapes—to paint the cards, and he got poets like Alfred Tennyson and Henry Wadsworth Longfellow to write the verses inside. The public clamored for each new release, and many women even recorded in their diaries how many "Prangs" they'd received that season. Prang's efforts to improve his product also made his cards more expensive. A Prang could cost as much as $1.75—a lot of money for the average worker who earned only about $1.50 a day.

But the exclusivity of Christmas cards couldn't last. The demand was just too high. And when German publishers flooded the market in the late 1880s with one-penny cards, Prang couldn't compete. By 1890 he was forced out of the Christmas card business.

The annual Christmas card ritual was firmly established in the United States, though. Homegrown publishers took over the business after World War I, and today more than 3,000 American card companies sell 2 billion Christmas cards every year.

Card Curiosities

- Only 12 of the cards made by artist John Calcott Horsley,

who designed the very first Christmas cards in 1843, exist today, and they're all in private collections. One of those originals sold at an auction in 2001 for $40,000, making it the most expensive Christmas card in the world.

- Postmen in Victorian England were popularly called "robins" because of their red uniforms, and Christmas cards of that era often showed a robin delivering mail.

- Kodak introduced the first photograph card in 1902.

- Dwight Eisenhower sent the first White House Christmas card in 1953 to 2,000 of his "personal" friends. (Today, the White House mails more than 1.6 million Christmas cards every year.)

- The average American family receives about 20 Christmas cards each year.

*   *   *

Mummy Christmas

In the 1860s, a shortage of linen and other raw materials caused by the Civil War led an enterprising paper manufacturer in Gardiner, Maine, to import Egyptian mummies by the shipload and use the linen coverings to make plain brown Christmas wrapping paper.

Diamond's Are a Kid's Best Friend

Some gift ideas for the kid who has absolutely everything.

Extremely Hot Wheels
Value: $140,000

Hot Wheels celebrated its 40th anniversary by introducing a diamond-encrusted car at the 2008 New York Toy Fair. Designed by celebrity jeweler Jason Arasheben, the car has 2,700 blue, black, and white diamonds dotting its 18-karat white gold frame. The blue diamonds re-create the trademark Hot Wheels Spectraframe blue paint, and black and white diamonds decorate the car's engine and underbelly. The brake lights are rubies. In 2008 proceeds from the auction of the car went to Big Brothers and Sisters of America.

Diamond Barbie
Value: $85,000

In 1999 Barbie turned 40. (Don't tell!) To celebrate the doll's birthday, Mattel worked with jewelers at DeBeers to design her a gown suitable for the occasion. The gown drips with

160 diamonds and is accessorized with white gold, making Barbie the talk of many towns when she toured major jewelers to celebrate her big day.

Golden Game Boy
Value: $25,000
The folks at Aspreys of London took it upon themselves to create the world's most expensive Game Boy. It's made of 18-karat gold, and diamonds border the display screen.

Jubilee Teddy Bear
Value: $85,000
What has fur spun from gold thread, a solid-gold mouth, and two eyes that sparkle with diamonds and sapphires? The Steiff teddy bear, of course. In 2005, to commemorate the company's 125th anniversary in the teddy bear–making business, Steiff built 125 jeweled bears, each with a 14-karat gold trademark Steiff button in its ear. One later sold at auction for $193,000!

* * *

Singing Like a Canary
If you get a speeding ticket around the holidays and end up in front of Tennessee judge Tom Dubois, you can "pay" the fine by singing a Christmas carol to the court.

Lost and Found

*'Tis the season for surprises. Witness these little mysteries
that found their resolution around the holidays.*

Lost: A Christmas card mailed on December 23, 1908, to
Elsa Johansson of Sweden.
Found: The card finally arrived in 1985.

Lost: A coin hidden in Christmas pudding was swallowed by
13-year-old Marie Hefferman on December 25, 1972.
Found: The coin reappeared in 1994 when Hefferman had a
coughing fit and spit it up.

Lost: James McDonnell of New York was in two car accidents in 1971 and suffered major head injuries. One day, he
told a friend he had a headache and then went for a walk. He
never came back.
Found: McDonnell returned on Christmas Day, 1985. He
told his wife Anne that the day he disappeared he "woke up"
in Philadelphia with no identification and no memory of his
past or who he was. He only knew his name was James. He
explained that he had taken the last name Peters from a store

sign and that for the last 14 years he'd been working as a postal supervisor. His memory returned when he bumped his head on Christmas Eve, and he went straight home to his old life in New York.

Lost: A New Year's greeting card from teenage diarist Anne Frank, mailed on December 31, 1937, to her friend Sanne Ledermann.

Found: On April 23, 2007, Dutch primary school teacher Paul van den Heuvel found the card in his parents' antique shop in the small town of Naarden-Vesting near Amsterdam. He was searching for material for a lesson on Anne Frank. Anne had written the card to her friend back in Holland while visiting her grandmother in Aachen, Germany, though how the card found its way to the antique shop remains a mystery.

Lost: A wild owl, nicknamed "Cheech the Screech," in December 2005.

Found: A Sarasota, Florida, couple found Cheech lounging on a branch when they went to trim their Christmas tree. When vets from a bird sanctuary removed the owl, they discovered that Cheech was high on marijuana. "Absolutely a first for me," said sanctuary spokesperson Jeff Dearing. "I've never had any owl or any other winged creature, for that matter, come in high." Once the vets determined the owl was OK, they released him back into the wild . . . on his own recognizance, of course.

Yuletide Yuks

Eat! Drink! And tell corny jokes!

Which of Santa's reindeer is bad-mannered?
Rude-olph.

What do you give a reindeer with an upset stomach?
Elk-a-seltzer.

What does Prancer want for Christmas?
A pony sleigh station.

What's red and goes "Ho! Ho! Ho! Plop?"
Santa laughing his head off.

What Christmas carol makes you thirsty?
"The First No Well"

Christmas Q & A

*For many Christmas lovers, these terms are
familiar, but their definitions aren't.*

Who was Good King Wenceslas?

The Good King Wenceslas who, as the song named for him
goes, "looked out on the Feast of Stephen" was not a king at
all, but the duke of Bohemia from AD 924 to 935. Wenceslas
tried to convert the Czechs to Christianity but was eventually
murdered by his heathen brother. After his death, legends
sprang up about his piety and kindness to the poor. Holy
Roman Emperor Otto I made him a king posthumously, and
the Catholic church granted him sainthood in 985. He's still
the patron saint of the Czechs, who call him Svaty Vaclav.

What is a *bûche de Noël*?

Usually made of sponge cake and crafted to look like a traditional Yule log, the *bûche de Noël* is a popular dessert, mostly
in France and Quebec. Most bakers decorate their *bûche de
Noëls* with chocolate buttercream frosting, fresh fruit, and an
evergreen sprig, but others get fancy—we found one recipe
that called for marzipan mushrooms.

What is wassail?

Wassail is a medieval beverage served hot and made of ale, wine, or hard cider. It's usually topped with beaten eggs or stale bread. The name comes from the Old Norse *ves heill*, meaning "in good health." It was a tradition to visit neighbors on Christmas Eve and drink a wassail to their health. Modern recipes for wassail use hot apple cider simmered with cinnamon and other spices.

Why do we eat mincemeat pie?

This practice dates back to the 16th century, when people believed that eating a small pie on each of the 12 days of Christmas would bring good luck in the New Year. Originally a way to preserve and extend the shelf life of meat by adding aromatic spices like cinnamon, nutmeg, and cloves, mincemeat evolved over time into the virtually meatless concoction it is today: a mélange of finely chopped (minced) fruits and spice combined with suet (animal fat). (It has always tasted much better than it sounds.)

*   *   *

The Name Game

Before Charles Dickens settled on Tiny Tim as the name for Bob Cratchit's son in A Christmas Carol, he considered three other names: Little Larry, Small Sam, and Puny Pete.

The Wizard's Christmas

Inventor Thomas Edison was called the "Wizard of Menlo Park," and here's a big reason why.

In 1879 passengers on trains traveling from New York to Philadelphia were in for an incredible sight. On those December nights, all of the towns the trains passed were bathed in darkness . . . except one. Menlo Park, New Jersey—home to Thomas Edison and his "invention factory"—sparkled with light.

Bright Idea

It was all part of Edison's plan to draw attention to himself and his inventions. "The Wizard of Menlo Park," as the press had dubbed him, worked on the stunt for months. He bragged that he intended to light whole cities with his electrical system and that it was only a matter of time until gaslight, which he called dirty and unsafe, became obsolete.

In the months leading up to Christmas 1879, Edison laid eight miles of underground wire across half a square mile of his Menlo Park laboratory property. His workmen planted rows of white, wired posts to hold the thousands of light-bulbs his factory had mass-produced. Glass globes covered the bulbs. The old library annex was converted into a central power station containing 11 generators. When the trains passed by on their way to New York or Philadelphia, Edison turned a wheel in the power station and flooded the barren fields with a brilliant array of twinkling streetlights.

In addition to the impressive outdoor display, hundreds of lamps installed in the homes, boardinghouses, and plant buildings of his New Jersey research facility sprang to life. It was the most incredible display of artificial light that the world had ever seen.

Twinkle, Twinkle

That Christmas season, Edison was the toast of two cities. Congressmen, dignitaries, bankers, stockbrokers, and celebrities traveled from New York and Philadelphia to New Jersey to see his "Fairy-land of Lights." Even actress Sarah Bernhardt came to visit and was dazzled by the display. The publicity stunt worked. He got the go-ahead to bring electricity to Manhattan.

Today New York, Tomorrow the World

Less than three years later, in 1882, Edison had installed a central generating station that was humming away on New York's Pearl Street. And as one last Christmas treat for the city's residents, Edward H. Johnson, a longtime associate of Edison's, put a Christmas tree in the window of his New York City home and decorated it with 80 red, white, and blue lights. The electric age had begun, and it all started with 1,000 sparkling lights in one small New Jersey town.

*   *   *

Let It Snow, Let It Snow, Let It Snow

If you're looking for a unique Christmas vacation, consider the city of Dubai in the United Arab Emrites. Typically one of the hottest places on earth, this desert city has recently become a ski bunny's paradise. Ski Dubai, an indoor resort, boasts five ski slopes (including one black diamond level for experienced skiers only), chairlifts, fake fir trees, and 6,000 tons of snow. The mock Swiss resort is 25 stories high and has perfect weather all the time. There are even several chalets inside where skiers can sip hot chocolate in front of a roaring fire. And for those visitors who don't come prepared, Ski Dubai rents skis, snowboards, coats, gloves, hats, and anything else they need to brave the indoor winter wonderland.

Christmas Toasts

At holiday dinners, someone always stands and offers a toast. Here are five of our favorites.

"Holly and ivy hanging up, and something good in every cup!"

—Irish

"A merry Christmas this December, to a lot of folks I don't remember."

—Franklin P. Adams, satirist

"May you live as long as you wish, and have all you wish for as long as you live."

—Irish

"Here's to the season when fowl murder promotes peace and goodwill."

—Anonymous

"If you can't be merry at Christmas, then you can drive the rest of us home when we are!"

—Unknown

Up, Up, and Away

For more than 80 years, the Macy's Thanksgiving Day Parade has launched the Christmas season with fabulous floats, marching bands, musical extravaganzas, and . . . balloons.

1924: Lions and Tigers and Santa, Oh My!

Macy's first parade was called "Macy's Christmas Parade." It featured Macy's employees dressed as clowns, cowboys, genies, knights, and princesses. It also included horse-drawn floats, lions and tigers from the Central Park Zoo, and, of course, Santa. A year later, party-sized balloon animals (filled with air and carried through the streets) took the place of real animals.

1927: It's a Gas!

Helium was introduced, and the balloons could fly high. First balloon star? Felix the Cat. Other balloons included a dragon, an elephant, and a toy soldier.

The same year, organizers released the balloons at the end of the parade. Unfortunately, the helium expanded, and four of them—including a 27-foot-tall toy soldier—exploded. (You'd think they wouldn't do that again, and yet . . .)

1929–1930: Hunting Season!

The balloons were still released, but they slowly leaked helium so they eventually came back to earth. They also had address labels and prizes offered to those who returned them. New Yorkers went wild trying to catch the giant balloons. Two tugboats nearly collided as they rushed to collect the dachshund balloon from the East River. (The boats survived, but the pup was toast.) Other balloons were returned to Macy's filled with bullet holes.

1932–1933: That Darn Cat!

A pilot tried to snag Felix the Cat, but Felix slammed into the plane's wing and was destroyed—and the plane nearly crashed. Another pilot sent his plane into a tailspin trying to retrieve a balloon over Long Island. Finally, Macy's officials had second thoughts about the release-and-catch policy and canceled it.

1934: Who's the Leader of the Club?

Mickey Mouse joined the parade . . . in the form of a 40-foot-tall balloon.

1941: Ho! Ho! Ow!

The Santa balloon had a round belly. Handlers thought it was great to bounce him up and down along the parade route. It wasn't. He exploded.

1942–1944: Parade Rest

The parade was canceled for the duration of World War II. All the balloons, including the 75-foot Uncle Sam, "gave their lives" (donated their rubber) to the war effort. Macy's employees chopped them up in a big ceremony.

1945: I'm Flying High

The war was over, and the balloons were back! The parade was televised for the first time, but it was broadcast only in New York City. It didn't go national until 1948.

1958: Lift and Separate

Due to a helium shortage, balloons were filled with air and suspended from cranes.

1971: Deflated

Strong winds forced the balloons to sit this parade out.

1985: It's Not Easy Being Green . . . and Wet

The Kermit the Frog balloon got so waterlogged from rain that handlers had to carry the big green guy through the streets.

1993: Sonic Boom

The Sonic the Hedgehog balloon slammed into a streetlight

and an off-duty policeman—and broke the officer's shoulder bone.

1997: It's a Twister

Gale-force winds wreaked havoc with the balloons. Sonic the Hedgehog lost his head. The Nestlé Nesquik Bunny lost an ear near Columbus Circle. Knife-wielding policemen were forced to deflate Barney and cut the tail off the Pink Panther to keep him under control. On 72nd Street, the Cat in the Hat balloon crashed into a lamppost, knocking debris into the crowd. Several people were injured, including a woman who remained in a coma for more than a month. (She lived.)

1998: We Need Rules

New York City imposed stricter guidelines: The parade could no longer include balloons more than 70 feet tall, 40 feet wide, or 78 feet long. (This forced several characters, Woody Woodpecker among them, into retirement.) City officials also decreed that balloons had to be grounded if the wind went above 23 mph.

2005: Melts on Your Head, Not in Your Hand

The 50-foot, 853-pound M&M balloon hit a streetlight and careened into two sisters, injuring them both.

2006: Blistering Barnacles!

The SpongeBob SquarePants balloon snagged a lamppost in Herald Square. As a police officer tried to release him, spectators chanted, "Free SpongeBob!"

Balloon Bits

- Macy's is second only to the U.S. government in helium consumption.

- It takes 400,000 cubic feet of helium to blow up 16 giant balloons.

- Average weight per balloon: 500 pounds.

- Average height: between five and six stories high.

- It takes an average of 2,000 handlers, or wranglers, to guide all of the balloons through the 43-block parade route.

- The largest balloon used in the parade was the 100-foot-long Superman, who first flew in 1939.

- The only balloon based on a real person was that of entertainer Eddie Cantor, launched in 1940.

- The first female balloon character was Olive Oyl, introduced in 1982.

Fractured Carols

We've all sung them, too. Here are some of our favorite misheard Christmas carol lyrics.

- Joy to the world, the Lord has gum!" ("Joy to the World")

- "We three kings of porridge and tar." ("We Three Kings")

- "Everybody knows a turkey, handsome Mr. Soul . . ." ("The Christmas Song")

- "Later on we'll perspire as we drink by the fire." ("Winter Wonderland")

- "Sleep in heavenly peas . . ." ("Silent Night")

- "Oh, what fun it is to ride with one horse, soap, and hay!" ("Jingle Bells")

- "With the jelly toast proclaim . . ." ("Hark, the Herald Angles Sing")

- "Good tidings we bring to you and your kid!" ("We Wish You a Merry Christmas")

- "Fleas naughty dog!" ("Feliz Navidad")

It Was a Very Good Year

It's taken a long time for the Christmas traditions we know and love to become popular. Here's how some of them got started.

AD 354
The first recorded Christmas celebration was held in Rome.

700
St. Boniface, an English missionary to Germany, held up an evergreen bough to symbolize Christ everlasting. According to legend, it was the first Christmas tree.

1200
European monks sang the first Christmas carols.

1610
Tinsel (made out of real silver) was invented in Germany, using machines to pull the silver into wafer-thin strips. The silver tarnished quickly in candlelight, though, so people tried using lead and tin before finally settling on aluminum foil and plastic in the mid 1900s.

1643

St. Jean de Brébeuf, a Jesuit missionary, wrote "The Huron Carol" in the Huron language. It was the first Christmas carol written in North America.

1670

A choirmaster in Cologne, Germany, bent sticks of candy into the familiar cane shape to represent a shepherd's crook. (The canes didn't get stripes until 1900.)

1843

The first Christmas card was published in London.

1850

A character in Harriet Beecher Stowe's story "The First Christmas of New England" made the first recorded complaint about the commercialization of Christmas.

1870

President Ulysses S. Grant made December 25 a holiday.

1939

Rudolph joined Dasher, Dancer, and the other reindeer on Santa's sleigh when copywriter Robert L. May introduced the character as part of a promotion for the Montgomery Ward department store.

1942

Bing Crosby recorded "White Christmas" in just 18 minutes. Crosby was not impressed with his performance, saying that "a jackdaw with a cleft palate" could have sung the song as well, but "White Christmas" went on to become the best-selling Christmas song of all time.

1984

Rock stars gathered to record "Do They Know It's Christmas?" The single sold more the 3.5 million copies and raised $18 million for African famine relief.

*   *   *

Tree Bits

- The United States' official Christmas tree is called the General Sherman Tree. It's a 300-foot tall giant sequoia located in California's King's Canyon National Park.

- Leading American Christmas tree producer: the state of Oregon. Farmers harvest more than 8 million trees there every year.

- Trees from Christmas tree farms are fuller than ones found in nature. That's because handlers clip the farmed trees' tops every spring to discourage them from growing up. This makes the trees grow more branches instead.

The Red Kettle

*The Salvation Army gave us two classic symbols
of charity: a bell ringer and a red kettle.*

A Promise Made . . .

In the winter of 1891, Captain Joseph McFee of the
Salvation Army was saddened by the number of homeless
people who roamed San Francisco. So he vowed to provide a
Christmas dinner for all of the city's poor. His only problem
was paying for it.

In trying to come up with a solution, Captain McFee
thought back to his sailing days in England and remembered
the large iron kettle that stood at Stage Landing, Liverpool.
It was called Simpson's Pot, and the sailors coming on or off
ships would toss in a coin to help feed the poor. McFee
wondered if a similar pot would work on the streets of San
Francisco.

. . . A Promise Kept

McFee placed the Salvation Army's first kettle—a red crab
pot on a tri-pod—at the Oakland Ferry Landing at the foot
of Market Street. He also posted a sign that read, "Keep the

Pot Boiling." It worked. Commuters on their way to and from the ferries dropped their spare change into the pot. By December 25, Captain McFee had raised enough cash to pay for the Christmas dinner.

The idea of using red kettles to collect donations to help the poor soon spread. By 1897 the kettles had found their way to Boston, where volunteers dressed in Santa suits stood next to the kettles and rang bells. That year, the combined nationwide effort paid for 150,000 Christmas dinners. Then, in 1901, red kettle donations funded the first massive "sit-down" dinner at Madison Square Garden in New York City.

Buddy, Can You Spare a Tooth?

Most donations take the form of nickels, dimes, and quarters. But over the years, bell ringers have reported some surprising gifts from passersby—a Krugerrand (a gold South African coin), diamond rings, even a pair of gold molars.

The kettles, too, have changed with the times. Some now have self-ringing bells, and others come equipped with credit-card machines. There's even one that comes in its own booth that broadcasts Christmas carols.

Ring Them Bells!

Today, money tossed into the Salvation Army's red kettles continues to bring Christmas dinners and holiday assistance—such as toys, coats, and rent and utility payments—to more than 6 million Americans. And the money raised in each community always goes to the people who live there. Meanwhile, the Red Kettle Campaign has circled the globe. Bell ringers and kettles can now be found in Korea, Japan, Chile, and many European countries.

Kettle Facts

- Kettles in the United States: 20,000

- Combined hours spent on bell ringing: 4,600,000

- Number of days the kettles are on display: 25

- Average amount of money collected per kettle each Christmas: $5,625

- Largest amount of money ever raised in a single year (2006): $118 million

- Number of Americans helped annually by the campaign: 35 million

*   *   *

A Note from Uncle John

Anyone can be a bell ringer. All you have to do is contact your local Salvation Army branch a month or so before Christmas and offer to volunteer.

They Wrote the Songs

*When it comes to writing a hit Christmas carol,
good ideas can come from the oddest places.*

Sing It, Cowboy!

Cowboy crooner Gene Autry was riding his horse Champion
in the annual Hollywood Christmas parade when he heard
kids shouting, "Here comes Santa Claus! Here comes Santa
Claus!" as Santa's sleigh rounded the corner behind him.
Before the parade was finished, Autry had written the lyrics
of his soon-to-be hit. Composer Oakley Haldeman added the
music, but the final ingredient didn't come until the recording session. Producer Art Satherley was clutching a cocktail
and leaning a little too close to the microphone when singer
Johnny Bond made a demo recording of "Here Comes Santa
Claus." Everyone agreed that Satherley's clinking ice cubes
sounded just like sleigh bells. Autry later used real sleigh bells
for his Columbia Records production in 1947, and it became
a Top 10 pop and country hit.

Tinkle Bells

Composer Ray Evans was inspired to write "Silver Bells" after hearing all those Salvation Army bell ringers standing outside department stores at Christmas. But according to Evans, the bells weren't always silver. They started out as "Tinkle Bells." When cowriter Jay Livingston told his wife about the song, she said, "Are you out of your mind? Do you know what the word 'tinkle' means? It is a child's slang for 'urinate.'" The bells promptly got a new name, and "Silver Bells" became an instant classic. Bob Hope and Marilyn Maxwell introduced the song in the 1951 movie *The Lemon Drop Kid*. Bing Crosby and Carol Richards then recorded it in 1952.

*   *   *

Holiday Hazards

According to England's Royal Society for the Prevention of Accidents, you better watch out for these hazards:

1. Trees: Nearly 34 percent of all Christmastime accidents involve trees—branches gouge eyes, people cut themselves with axes, and decorators fall off of chairs.

2. Candles injure about 900 people every year.

3. Christmas lights account for 12 percent of accidents.

4. Ornaments: About 500 toddlers bite into ornaments annually.

5. Cooking: Hot grease, boiling water, and electric carving knives injure many people every Christmas.

Garage Sale Queens

*Every year, Shaela Wilson and her friends bring warmth
and comfort to those whom Santa has forgotten.*

The First Noel

In 1991, Shaela Wilson was having a really tough year. She
was an out-of-work single mother living near Austin, Texas,
who was struggling to make ends meet. If it hadn't been for
a gift of $50 from her grandparents, there would have been
little for Wilson and her six-year-old daughter Breezy to look
forward to on Christmas morning.

But Breezy wasn't thinking about toys. She was con-
cerned about her father. The last anyone had heard of him,
he was living on the streets, and the thought of her dad cold
and alone on Christmas morning really worried the little girl.
"The best way to allay Breezy's concerns was to show her that
there are good people who are willing to help those less for-
tunate," Wilson said. Two of those good people would be
Shaela and Breezy.

So they took the gift of $50 and used it to buy eight
blankets. On the Saturday morning just before Christmas
Eve, they drove to the Warehouse District in Austin, where

many homeless people hung out. Holding two bags of blankets in one hand and her daughter's hand in the other, Wilson approached a man standing outside the Helping Our Brothers Out shelter for the homeless and offered him a blanket. Suddenly, 20 more men clamoring for blankets surrounded the pair. Wilson dropped the blankets, grabbed her daughter, and ran for their car. She was about to apologize for putting Breezy in such danger when the little girl looked up at her mother and said, "Mommy, that was the best part of my Christmas." And that's how the Wilsons' Annual Homeless Christmas Project was born.

Gathering the Goods

Now, more than 15 years later, Shaela, Breezy, a friend named Kate Murphy, and some devoted helpers deliver more than blankets to the homeless. Shaela Wilson starts stocking up on clothes, toiletries, and other items at the beginning of January. She and Murphy put on their "uniforms"—rhinestone tiaras, purple tennis shoes, and purple t-shirts (with their titles of "Garage Sale Queen" emblazoned in gold).

Nearly every weekend, the women set out before sunrise to scour local garage sales. When the people holding the sales hear about the cause, often donate sleeping bags, blankets, and coats. Other people give new items. By the time the holidays roll around, the Garage Sale Queens have amassed several carloads of goods for the homeless.

The Queens Make the Holiday Scene

Two weekends before Christmas, Shaela and Breezy Wilson tell their contacts on the street to spread the word: the Garage Sale Queens are coming to town. Then, on the last Saturday before Christmas Eve, the Queens and their friends deliver the goodies to a crowd of waiting homeless men, women, and children. Today, the scene is less chaotic than it was that first year—the people take only what they need, wish each other a Merry Christmas, and then return to Austin's streets.

*   *   *

Christmas Game: Snapdragon

Despite some burned fingers and lips, Snapdragon (or Flapdragon, as it was also called) was one of 19th-century America's most popular Christmas party games.

- **Supplies:** A wide shallow bowl, currants, brandy, and a box of matches.

- **How to play:** Place a bowl full of currants drenched in brandy in the center of table. Turn off the lights and drop a lighted match into the bowl. While the brandy is burning, players challenge each other to pluck a flaming currant out of the bowl and pop it into their mouths.

Dear Santa

Every kid knows that Santa lives at the North Pole. Here are a few of the 120,000 letters he's received, courtesy of the U.S. Postal service in North Pole, Alaska.

Dear Santa,

Why can't people know when you're in the house? Can the reindeer talk? . . . Can you leave me a sleigh bell off your harness please!

—Lane

Dear Santa,

I want a big bear hug . . . I wish I could see you but I am always sleeping.

—Taylor

Dear Santa,

I would like to get things for my family but I have no money. I was hoping that you can help me by getting them . . . and just put my name on them so they know I am thoughtful.

—*Bethany*

Dear Santa,
Please forgive me for my wrong mistakes. Me and my brother DO believe in you. We will have some YUMMY cookies waiting for you!

—*Alyssa*

*   *   *

Santa's Helpers

North Pole, Alaska, local Gabby Gaborik is one of 45 volunteers who work as a Santa's helper each year opening crates full of letters. During the Christmas rush, as many as 12,000 come each day. In his 10 years on the job, Gaborik has seen every kind of request, including one boy asking for his own personal elf and a woman asking if Santa could help her get pregnant. His favorite letter was one that arrived with a Michigan postmark but had no stamp or return address. Inside was a $1,000 money order and this note: "If you are who you say you are, you'll put this to good use."

Santa's helpers used the money to buy stamps so they could send out replies from their boss to all of the children.

The Christmas Panto

*You may never have heard of it, but this holiday show is
as much a tradition in the United Kingdom as*
The Nutcracker *is in the United States.*

They call it "British pantomime," but it has nothing to
do with guys in white face performing mime in the
park. "Panto," as it's known today, is a style of theater with
roots in the Italian Renaissance when comedy troupes traveled throughout Europe. Since their audiences spoke many
different languages, the players developed a performing style
characterized by easily recognizable characters, broad slap-
stick, and lots of physical movement. In England, panto
troupes sprang up in the early 1700s as locals came together
during the holidays to entertain family and friends.

Evil Queens, Ugly Stepsisters

Panto scripts have stock characters who appear in every show.
There's the Dame (a man dressed as a woman who wears
absurdly large wigs), the Principal Boy (played by a young
woman), the villain, and clowns like the Ugly Sisters (usually
played by men). This cross-dressing tradition was pioneered

in the 19th century by the "King of the Clowns," Joseph Grimaldi, whose performances as Dame Cecily Suet, an enormous spoon-wielding cook, brought down houses throughout Great Britain.

In panto, the jokes are bad and full of double entendres, the songs are often cobbled together from current hits, and there's lots of audience participation. If an actor onstage declares, "Oh, yes, I will!" the audience responds, "Oh, no, you won't!" And everyone boos the villain, of course.

Fractured Fairy Tales

Almost every town in Great Britain produces a panto at Christmastime, and the story is always a twist on a childhood favorite like *Cinderella*, *Aladdin*, or *Snow White*. But pantos are not just for amateur performers. For the last 100 years, large professional theaters have vied with each other to attract stars who will be big audience draws. (In 2005 Sir Ian McKellan was a mammoth success as the Widow Twankey in *Aladdin* at London's Old Vic theater.)

It's hard to exaggerate the fierce loyalty Brits feel toward this tradition. Many of them consider seeing panto to be one of the most sacred rites of childhood and as much a part of the holidays as roast beef with Yorkshire pudding, the Queen's Christmas Message, and Boxing Day. Even playwright George Bernard Shaw quipped, "A child who has not seen a pantomime is a public danger."

Crazy Days of Christmas

Let's face it. The holidays can be stressful. And when they get stressed, people can act a little, well . . . nutty.

Step on It!

On December 3, 2006, David Allen Rodgers—the driver of the Steppin' Out Dance Studio float in the annual Christmas parade in Anderson, South Carolina—suddenly pulled out of the lineup and sped past the float in front of him . . . with 18 people still onboard! While the dancers held on for dear life, one managed to call 911 and alert the police. Rodgers drove down Main Street, ran a red light, and led police on a three-mile chase. He was finally arrested and charged with 36 offenses, including driving under the influence, assaulting a police officer, and 18 counts of kidnapping.

Santa and the Streaker

A few days before Christmas in 2006, Santa Claus was just coming home from a tough day at the toy workshop (OK, he was really at the mall) outside of Damascus, Virginia. But then what to his wondering eyes did appear but a man stripping off all of his clothes and throwing them out the car window. The man then drove into town, leaped out of his car, and ran stark naked through Damascus. Santa (who requested that his identity be withheld) told Virginia's Channel 11 News, "Santa sees you when you're sleeping, he sees when you're awake, and he sees when you're naked coming down the street." (Police Chief Tony Richardson said the distressed streaker turned out to be a 35-year-old man who had been to the dentist and taken too many pain pills.)

Santa Gets Mugged

Who knew that being Santa could be such a hazardous occupation? Stefan Stetler, 31, from Wiesbaden, Germany, learned the hard way that he should leave his work at work. He was still in his Santa suit and toting a bag of presents as he waited for the train home when he made the mistake of jokingly asking two commuters to "tell Santa what they want for Christmas." The men, who were apparently stressed out from a full day of Christmas shopping, were not amused. They grabbed Stetler's sack of presents and beat him over the head with it. Stetler told police that around this time of year, shoppers do get testy: "I should have known better," he confessed. "But come on, who beats up Santa Claus?"

*   *   *

Best-selling Christmas trees: Scotch pine and Douglas fir.

Christmas in the Colonies

Christmas was banned in most of New England during the 17th century—even making Christmas cookies was illegal. The holiday remained unpopular there until the 1800s. But some American colonists still managed to put the "Merry" in Christmas.

The Great Christmas Ban

The Puritans outlawed Christmas in the late 1600s because they considered it unholy: December 25 had been arbitrarily assigned as Christ's birthday and held no religious significance for them. Also, Christmas celebrations were usually rowdy affairs that included drinking and overeating, of which the Puritans disapproved. Plus, the Puritans were trying to distance themselves from the Anglican Church of England, so renouncing one of that church's main holidays seemed like a good way to do it.

The ban lasted for only about 22 years, but it took a long time for Northerners to embrace the holiday. Bostonians didn't start to celebrate until the 1800s.

The Southern colonies, though, took a different

approach. In particular, the people in Virginia (most of whom were Anglican and, thus, didn't need to disassociate from the Church of England) held on to their old-world traditions and continued to be enthusiastic about the holiday. Here are three ways colonial Virginians made merry:

- Virginians liked to celebrate, but going to church remained an important part of their Christmas tradition. "Sticking the church" meant decorating the sanctuary with greenery on Christmas Eve. Colonists hung garlands of holly, ivy, mountain laurel, and mistletoe from the eaves, walls, pillars, and galleries.

- Young Virginians liked to "shoot in the Christmas" by firing off rifles and pistols on Christmas morning. Others banged on pots and pans to welcome in the holiday.

- During the early 18th century, students at Williamsburg's College of William and Mary ushered in their Christmas break with a ceremonial lockout called "barring out" the teachers. The students nailed their classroom doors shut in the middle of the night to prevent classes from taking place. In 1702, when the college's founder, Reverend James Blair, tried to force his way into the school, students fired their pistols and shouted, "For God's sake, sir, don't offer to come in, for we have shot, and shall certainly fire at any one that first enters." Blair wisely beat a strategic retreat.

Five More Little-Known Christmas Films

*We began this list on page 31, and we
bet you don't know these movies either.*

3 Godfathers (1948)

Here's an oddity—a Christmas movie with no snow. Set in
the Old West and directed by John Ford, this film stars John
Wayne, Harry Carey Jr., and Pedro Armendariz as a trio of
outlaws who promise a dying mother (Mildred Natwick)
they'll take care of her infant baby . . . on Christmas,
naturally. As the three bad guys ("stunt doubles" for the
Three Wise Men) cope with the challenges of raising a child,
they find redemption for their lives of crime through the
power of love. The movie was remade in 1987 as *Three Men
and a Baby*—minus the religious overtones.

The Great Rupert (1950)

The official star of this film is funnyman Jimmy Durante,
but the show-stealer is a dancing squirrel named Rupert (a
product of stop-motion animation). With the help of some
timely cash, the squirrel rescues Durante's family from a grim

Christmas and becomes their guardian angel. The movie features Durante singing "Jingle Bells" and other familiar Christmas songs in his inimitable style.

The Lemon Drop Kid (1951)

Damon Runyon supplied the story for what turned out to be one of Bob Hope's finest film roles. Hope plays the Lemon Drop Kid, a two-bit hustler in debt to a gangster who wants his money back right away. So Hope cons his fellow con artists into posing as street-corner Santas to raise the money for him. Along the way, the movie features the premiere of the classic holiday song "Silver Bells."

We're No Angels (1955)

How this wonderful comedy fell off the classic Christmas movie list is hard to understand. Humphrey Bogart, Peter Ustinov, and Aldo Ray play escaped convicts who descend on a hapless storekeeper at Christmas and intend to rob him. Instead, they get involved in the man's struggle to keep his landlord from throwing the storekeeper's family out on the street. Sentimental but not corny, the film humanizes the cons without stripping them of their toughness. As Bogie's character says, "We came here to rob them and that's what we're gonna do—beat their heads in, gouge their eyes out, slash their throats. Soon as we wash the dishes." Happy Holidays!

A Midwinter's Tale (1995)

This most recent addition to this list is probably the best. Written and directed by British theatrical wunderkind Kenneth Branagh, it's a bittersweet tale of struggling actors who try to rescue their careers by mounting a production of *Hamlet* in a small English town. At first, they squabble and bicker until the director throws in the towel in despair. But everything comes together for a (mostly) triumphant performance on Christmas Eve. Full of stock characters (the Old Ham, the Flamboyant Queen, the Egomaniacal Director), the movie transcends all the clichés to paint a charming portrait of humanity in all its foibles.

*   *   *

A Hero's Holiday

Every Christmas since 1992, Merrill Worcester of the Worcester Wreath Company in Harrington, Maine, has donated 5,000 wreaths to be placed on the graves of the U.S. soldiers buried at Arlington Cemetery in Virginia. Worcester and dozens of volunteers drive the wreaths from Maine in trucks and trailers, and then lay them on the graves personally.

Christmas Curmudgeons

The holidays aren't all serious.

"Santa Claus has the right idea: Visit people once a year."
—Victor Borge

"In the old days, it was not called the Holiday Season; the Christians called it 'Christmas' and went to church; the Jews called it 'Hanukkah' and went to synagogue; the atheists went to parties and drank. People passing each other on the street would say 'Merry Christmas!' or 'Happy Hanukkah!' or (to the atheists) 'Look out for the wall!'"
—Dave Barry

"The three stages of a man's life: He believes in Santa Claus. He doesn't believe in Santa Claus. He is Santa Claus."
—Unknown

"Roses are reddish / Violets are bluish / If it weren't for Christmas / We'd all be Jewish."
—Benny Hill

"Once again we find ourselves enmeshed in the Holiday Season, that very special time of year when we join with our loved ones in sharing centuries-old traditions such as trying to find a parking space at the mall. We traditionally do this in my family by driving around the parking lot until we see a shopper emerge from the mall, then we follow her, in very much the same spirit as the Three Wise Men, who 2,000 years ago followed a star, week after week, until it led them to a parking space."

—*Dave Barry*

*   *   *

He's Making a List

On January 7, 1759, George Washington married Martha Custis, a widow with two young children: John Parke Custis (age five) and Martha Parke Custis (age three). The following Christmas their new dad wrote out a Christmas list of presents for them. Here are some of the gifts:

A bird on Bellows	Household Stuff
A Cuckoo	A Prussion Dragoon
A turnabout Parrot	A Tunbridge Tea Sett
A Grocers Shop	A neat dress'd Wax
An Aviary	Baby

Peace on Earth

Even in the madness of World War I, there was "peace on earth and good will toward men" . . . for a little while.

It began on Christmas Eve 1914. The war had reached a stalemate: neither the Allied (British, French, and Belgian) nor German armies could pierce each other's line to seize the advantage. Troops were hunkered down in trenches all along the 500-mile western front, reduced to taking potshots at each other across No Man's Land, a barbed wire and the mine-filled space between their lines. Soldiers on both sides were muddy, cold, and homesick.

Singalong

That night, the Allied soldiers near Ypres, Belgium, noticed a strange phenomenon. Clusters of tiny lights appeared above the German trenches. At first, the Allies were suspicious, fearing that a sneak attack was about to take place. But by the time they realized they were looking at Christmas trees lit with candles, the sound of men singing "Stille Nacht" ("Silent Night") began wafting across No Man's Land. When the Germans finished singing their carol, the Allies responded with one of their own, "O Come All Ye Faithful." The Germans joined in for the chorus. The singing went back and forth for hours in the dark.

Band of Brothers

With the dawn came a spontaneous truce, instigated primarily by the Germans, who held up signs in broken English that said, "You no fight, we no fight." All along the battle line at Ypres, German and Allied soldiers holding white flags edged out of their trenches and moved to meet their enemies.

They shook hands and exchanged gifts of cigarettes, brandy, sausages, chocolate, and newspapers. In some places, both sides got down to the grim business of burying the dead who'd fallen in No Man's Land. Soldiers showed each other photos of loved ones and snipped buttons off their coats to swap as souvenirs. A soldier who was a barber in civilian life set up "shop" in No Man's Land, offering a trim to men from either side. "What a sight," wrote British corporal John Ferguson. "Here we were laughing and chatting to men whom only a few hours before we were trying to kill."

According to the official war diary of Germany's 133rd Saxon Regiment, a Scottish soldier caused a stir when he brought out a soccer ball. Delighted soldiers began kicking the ball around in an impromptu game. Helmets were set on the frozen ground to outline the goals and sidelines, and the "international friendly" match was on. The German war diarist recorded that "Fritz" edged "Tommie" 3–2.

All Good Things End

As quickly as it began, the truce evaporated. When the midwinter light faded, soldiers drifted back behind their own lines and into their trenches and bunkers. Percy Jones, a veteran of England's Westminster Regiment, remarked later, "Altogether we had a great day with our enemies, and parted with much hand-shaking and mutual goodwill."

Then it was back to the business at hand. One of the officers—no one seems to remember whether it was a German or an Allied soldier—fired three shots in the air with his revolver, as if to signal the official end of the unofficial truce. The hostilities promptly resumed in full force. The Great War lasted for three more Christmases, but there were no more truces until peace came in 1918.

*　　*　　*

About 70 percent of people give their pets Christmas presents.

Thinking Outside the Christmas Box

This do-it-yourself author scored big.

Richard Paul Evans did not set out to become a best-selling author. But in 1992, Evans made a run for the Utah state legislature and lost by 100 votes. Suddenly, he was without a job and, for the first time in his adult life, had time on his hands. So he decided to write a book as a Christmas gift for his two daughters. Once Evans put pen to paper, it took him just six weeks to write *The Christmas Box*.

The Big Idea

Evans wrote constantly, even waking up in the middle of the night to jot down ideas. Once he wrote an entire chapter on some paper he found in his car. The story just came to him. It was about a widow named Mary and the family who moves in with her. The husband finds an antique box containing objects that reveal Mary's unending love for her daughter Andrea, who died in infancy.

When Evans finished the book, he made 20 copies of it,

which he passed out to his family and friends. The next day his brother called and said, "That book changed my life." Within a month, the 20 copies had been passed around more than 160 times. A stranger even called Evans to tell him how meaningful the story was.

Never Give Up

Emboldened by this support, Evans submitted his book to publishers. None were interested because conventional wisdom said that adult Christmas stories didn't sell. But Evans kept trying. He and his wife put their life savings into self-publishing 9,000 copies. They hit another wall when bookstore chains refused to carry *The Christmas Box* unless it came from a distributor. So Evans contacted a distributor and sent him the book. The distributor loved it and agreed to carry it.

Sales took off. All 9,000 copies sold quickly, and Evans printed 20,000 more. By mid-December 1993, bookstores were besieged with so many requests that they had to run advertisements saying the book was sold out. It seemed everyone wanted *The Christmas Box*. At one store, two women even got into a fistfight over the last copy.

The Big Time

The following year, Evans released the book nationally, and by December 1, 1994, more than 250,000 copies had been sold. *People* magazine ran a feature on *The Christmas Box* phenomenon, and Katie Couric interviewed Evans on *The Today Show*. By Christmas Eve, the book was #2 on the *New York Times* best-seller list.

Now the publishing houses were definitely interested. An auction among major publishers resulted in Simon & Schuster winning the rights to publish the hardcover version of *The Christmas Box*—for $4.5 million.

Evans held on to the paperback rights, though, and at Christmas in 1995, he decided to publish the paperback version of his book at the same time that Simon & Schuster published the hardcover version. This won him a "first"— *The Christmas Box* became the only book to top both the hardcover and paperback best-seller lists. Today, it has sold more than 8 million copies in 16 languages and 40 countries.

Christmas Box Angel

These days, Evans mostly wears his author hat. He has written 11 more books, all of which have been best-sellers. When he's not writing, though, he spends his earnings helping others. He commissioned the Christmas Box Angel Memorial, a statue of an angel set in the Salt Lake City Cemetery, where people can go for solace after the loss of a child. There are now Christmas Box Angels in cemeteries across the United States. And in 1997, Evans founded the Christmas Box House International, an organization that has provided shelter and protective services to more than 16,000 abused and neglected children.

Naughty or Nice?

We see you when you're sleeping. We know when you're awake . . .

Naughty: Brandi Ervin, South Carolina
What Santa Saw: In 2006 Brandy Ervin had her son (age 12) arrested for unwrapping his Christmas present, a Nintendo Game Boy, without her permission. He was charged with petty larceny. (Santa understands holidays are stressful and kids need to follow the rules but feels arrest is a little extreme.) The charges were eventually dropped.

Nice: Woman (identity unknown) in a red Honda, California
What Santa Saw: Every Christmas, this woman pays the toll for the six cars behind her on the San Francisco Bay Bridge.

Naughty: Robert William Handley, Ohio
What Santa Saw: Robert Handley wanted to legally change his name to Santa Claus. Why? He's jolly and round and has a snow-white beard and hair. He also wears wire-rimmed glasses. Everyone always called him "Santa" anyway, so he wanted to make it official. The judge denied his request, saying, "The petitioner seeks to take not only the name of

Santa Claus, but also to take on the identity of Santa Claus. Although thousands of people every year do take on the identity of Santa Claus around Christmas, the court believes it would be very misleading to the children in the community . . . to approve the applicant's name change petition."

Nice: Helen Tapp, Florida

What Santa Saw: In December 2005, Helen Tapp and her children learned that many families in New Orleans whose lives were destroyed by Hurricane Katrina weren't going to be able to celebrate Christmas. Determined to help, the single mother and her four children put a sign in the front yard that read "Santa, give our gifts to Katrina kids." Then Tapp sent the kids' gifts to four children in New Orleans.

Nice: Jay Frankston, California

What Santa Saw: From 1982 to 1994, Jay Frankston sorted through the stacks of letters to Santa Claus buried in the dead-letter room at his local postoffice and found the letters from kids who were genuinely in need (like a little girl who wanted a blanket for her mother, or a boy who didn't want to be lonely on Christmas). Frankston would send each child a telegram saying, "Got your letter. Will be at your house on Christmas Day. Santa." Then, on Christmas morning, Frankston dressed as Santa and visited the home of each child, bringing gifts for the whole family.

Merry Christmas: From Irving, Felix, and Mel

We found this fact ironic and remarkable: Jewish songwriters composed more than half of the 25 most popular Christmas songs.

It's hard to imagine the holidays without music, especially classics like "White Christmas" and "Rudolph the Red-Nosed Reindeer." We knew that many of those beloved tunes were written by some of the greatest songwriters in history: Irving Berlin, in particular. But we were surprised to discover that Jewish composers (in some cases, along with their non-Jewish colleagues) wrote 13 of the American Society of Composers, Authors and Publishers' top 25 Christmas songs. Take a look at the songs those men came up with.

#1: "Winter Wonderland"

"Winter Wonderland" is one of the two oldest songs on the list, but it only became the number-one most popular Christmas tune for the first time in 2007. Written by Felix Bernard and Richard B. Smith (who probably wasn't Jewish) in 1934, it was an instant success for Guy Lombardo and his Royal Canadians. Later recordings by the Andrews Sisters and Perry Como made it a holiday staple, but the most recent version by the Eurythmics in 1987 brought the song its resurgent popularity.

#2: "The Christmas Song" ("Chestnuts Roasting on an Open Fire")

Immortalized by Nat King Cole, this song was written in 1945 by Mel Tormé and Robert Wells. The pair wrote it during a July heat wave in Toluca Lake, California. Tormé later said that it was a way "to stay cool by thinking cool." The song took just 45 minutes to compose.

#4: "Santa Claus Is Coming to Town"

J. Fred Coots was the songwriting partner of Haven Gillespie. In 1934 Gillespie showed Coots the lyrics, and Coots came up with the tune in just 15 minutes. Soon after, the pair convinced popular entertainer Eddie Cantor to premiere the song on his radio show. It was an overnight sensation—100,000 sheet music orders came in the next morning.

#5: "White Christmas"

In 1940 Irving Berlin (who composed everything from "God Bless America" to "Puttin' on the Ritz") was staying at a hotel in Arizona when he got the idea for this song. He stayed up all night to complete it and told his secretary in the morning, "Grab your pen and take down this song. I just wrote the best song I've ever written—hell, I just wrote the best song that anybody's ever written." He may be right. It's the most-recorded holiday song, with more than 500 versions.

#6: "Let It Snow! Let It Snow! Let It Snow!"

Sammy Cahn (lyrics) and Jule Styne (music) wrote "Let It Snow!" in 1945 as paean to winter weather. Cahn later won four Oscars for other lyrics and was a favorite songwriter of Frank Sinatra. Styne scored big on Broadway with *Gentlemen Prefer Blondes*, *Gypsy*, and *Funny Girl*.

#8: "Sleigh Ride"

Leroy Anderson, who was not Jewish, wrote this in 1946 as an instrumental piece for the Boston Pops orchestra. Mitchell Parish, who was, wrote the lyrics we sing today. Parish is best remembered for writing the lyrics to "Stardust," "Deep Purple," and "Sophisticated Lady."

For the rest of the list, turn to page 151.

*　　*　　*

"Christmas is a time when you get homesick—even when you're home."　　　　　　　　　　　*—Carol Nelson*

Christmas in Space

*When you're aboard a ship in the cold, dark vacuum
of space where eggnog and crackling fires are
far away, you have to be creative
to celebrate the holidays.*

- The first astronauts to spend Christmas in orbit were the three men on *Apollo 8* in 1968. William Anders, James Lovell, and Frank Borman made history when they became the first to orbit the moon while feasting on . . . fruitcake!

- The last crew to visit Skylab, a short-term U.S. space station, spent 84 days in space before returning to Earth on February 8, 1974. Astronauts Gerald Carr, William Pogue, and Edward Gibson decked the halls of their little corner of the universe with a Christmas tree made out of empty food cans.

- In 1996 astronaut John Blaha and cosmonauts Valery Korzun and Alexander Kaleri celebrated the Yuletide season while orbiting Earth aboard the Russian Mir space station. Christmas dinner included a feast of "traditional cakes and other dishes, lamb, pork, and a wonderful dessert, as well as Italian food—macaroni and cheese, and other things."

- The International Space Station celebrated its first Christmas in 2000. Astronaut Bill Shepherd and Cosmonauts Yuri Gidzenko and Sergei Krikalev spent the day opening gifts, talking to their families, and dining on rehydrated turkey. Alcohol was off-limits to Shepherd—NASA forbids it—but the cosmonauts celebrated with a little brandy.

- For Christmas 2001 the *Expedition 4* crew (Yury Onufrienko, Daniel Bursch, and Carl Walz) spent the holidays doing what most college students do: sleeping, eating, watching movies, and talking on the phone.

- In 2002 the crewmembers of *Expedition 6* (Ken Bowersox, Nikolai Budarin, and Don Pettit) created a Christmas Twinkie "cake" shaped like a candycane and covered with red and white frosting.

Decorating No-No's

Decking the halls in microgravity 230 miles above Earth while speeding along at 17,500 mph is not an easy thing to do. Here are the top three decorating don'ts at the International Space Station:

1. No fresh pine Christmas tree: They're too dangerous. The

needles could float away and poke astronauts in the eye. As Mission Control points out, "It's a safety issue."

2. Absolutely no Christmas cookies for Santa: One bite of a cookie would fill the space station with a thick cloud of cookie crumbs. And you can forget the glass of cold milk, too; zero gravity means milk droplets floating everywhere.

3. Decorating with baubles and tinsel? Forget it. Tinsel wouldn't look right anyway, sticking out in all directions except down. And the baubles would just float away.

* * *

Space-Age Santa

On December 25, 1968, *Apollo 8* Astronauts James Lovell, Frank Borman, and William Anders emerged from the dark side of the moon. Here's Lovell's transmission with mission control in Houston:

> Lovell: . . . we have a bogey at 10 o'clock high.
> Mission Control: Is that the booster or is that an actual sighting?
> Lovell: We have several . . . actual sightings.
> Mission Control: Estimated distance or size?
> Lovell: We also have the booster in sight . . .
> Lovell: Mission Control, please be informed, there is a Santa Claus.

The Real Scrooge?

This Dickens character may have been inspired by a real guy.

Ebenezer Scrooge, from Charles Dickens's novel *A Christmas Carol*, was so heartless and money-grubbing that the word "Scrooge" has now come to mean "miser." But according to Sjef de Jong, a Dutch academic, Scrooge may have been inspired by the real life of Gabriel de Graaf, a 19th-century gravedigger who lived in Holland.

Most literary scholars agree that the character of Scrooge was an expansion of an earlier Dickens character: Gabriel Grub, from *The Pickwick Papers*. And Gabriel Grub was a lot like Gabriel de Graaf. Grub was a gravedigger who loathed Christmas. While digging a grave one Christmas Eve, though, Grub is kidnapped by goblins who show him visions of human suffering tempered by acts of kindness and generosity. This causes Grub to have a change of heart.

Plus, the real-life De Graaf, a drunken curmudgeon obsessed with money, disappeared one Christmas Eve, leaving only an empty bottle of gin in an open grave. Years later, he reappeared as a changed man, saying that dwarves had helped him alter his wicked ways. Sure sounds a lot like Scrooge.

If You Build It . . .

*On page 22, we discussed the history of gingerbread.
Now, take a look at some of the incredible things
people make with the tasty treat.*

The Bakers Grimm

Forming people and houses out of gingerbread has its roots
in Europe. In the 16th century, Queen Elizabeth I of
England gave her guests gingerbread likenesses of themselves
as gifts. And making gingerbread houses became popular in
the early 1800s after the 1812 publication of the Brothers
Grimm fairytale "Hansel and Gretel." In the story, the lost
children come upon a gingerbread house covered in frosting
and candy . . . and they start to nibble. Of course, it's a
witch's house, and the tale turns dark for the kids, but this
magical moment in children's literature kicked off a craze for
gingerbread houses.

Soon bakers all over Germany were delighting their
customers with edible houses called *hexenhaeusle* (witches'
houses) or *knusperhaeuschen* (houses for nibbling). When
Germans immigrated to the United States, they brought the
tradition with them, and Americans started making elaborate

gingerbread Christmas decorations. German immigrant children even built foot-high gingerbread people—complete with iced buttons and big smiles—and stood them in their homes' windows to entertain passersby.

In the nearly two centuries since, making a gingerbread house has become a popular Christmas tradition. And in some cases, the decorators go all out. The annual National Gingerbread Competition in Asheville, North Carolina, attracts bakers from all over the United States. Floridian Patricia Howard took home the grand prize title in 2007 with a brick gingerbread castle complete with wreaths, trees, a swinging gate, and turrets. Here are some more amazing gingerbread creations.

Biggest Gingerbread House

According to *Guinness World Records*, Roger Pelcher is the architect of the biggest gingerbread house. He built it in 2006 at Minnesota's Mall of America—the biggest mall in the United States. Standing 64 feet tall, the 1,496 square foot culinary delight took nine days to put together and required 14,250 pounds of gingerbread, 4,750 pounds of icing, and more than a ton of candy. It also included a gingerbread factory and animated worker elves.

Biggest Gingerbread Village

In 2002 a German baker named Sven Grumbach decided to

think bigger than making a mere gingerbread house. He built an entire gingerbread village, re-creating the East German town of Rostock (where he lives) as it was before Allied bombs destroyed it in World War II. (Grumbach used 16th century pictures as inspiration.) The village required 2,400 eggs, 1,760 pounds of flour, 880 pounds of almonds, 175 pounds of raisins, and 705 pounds of honey. It covered more than 4,300 square feet and contained hundreds of homes and shops.

Biggest Gingerbread Man

In 2006, Smithville, Texas, was home to the world's largest gingerbread man. He stood 25 feet tall, was 10 feet wide, and was made from 1,000 pounds of batter. Cen-Tex Marine Fabricators—a local company that makes manholes and hatches for ships—created the giant mold, which held about 1,000 pounds of batter. Townspeople then barbecued the big guy over an open flame as part of their annual Festival of Lights celebration.

After making sure their efforts had won them a place in *Guinness World Records*, the citizens of Smithville ate their man. According to one diner, he "went real good with barbe-cued deer."

Turn to page 141 for the story of the White House gingerbread tradition.

Old Song, New Tradition

Every January 1 at the stroke of midnight, revelers in English-speaking countries around the world sing "Auld Lang Syne" to ring in the New Year. But why?

A Poetic Coincidence

In 1788 poet Robert Burns sent a copy of "Auld Lang Syne" to the *Scots Musical Museum*, a magazine dedicated to preserving Scottish heritage. He included this comment: "The following song, an old song, of the olden times, and which has never been in print, nor even in manuscript until I took it down from an old man's singing, is enough to recommend any air."

Auld lang syne can be translated as "old long since" or "old times gone." Its words belonged to Burns, but the tune was an ancient Scottish folk song. It was published after Burns's death in 1796, and although it remained a much-loved tune often sung at reunions, it was seldom associated with New Year's Eve celebrations.

One Heck of a Guy

Fast forward to New Year's Eve 1929. Guy Lombardo and his

orchestra the Royal Canadians were broadcasting live from the Roosevelt Hotel in New York City. Lombardo would later say that it was coincidence, but just seconds after the clock struck midnight, the band played "Auld Lang Syne." The song caught on with the listening audience, and for almost 50 years, Lombardo's rendition of "Auld Lang Syne" was a staple of New Year's Eve broadcasts on radio and television. By the time the bandleader died in 1977, the song had become the tradition we know today.

*   *   *

A Season of Giving

By Christmas 1864, the people living outside Savannah, Georgia, were near starvation. The city proper had thus far been spared devastation, but both the Union and Confederate armies had stripped the outskirts of most of their resources. But even as the Civil War dragged on, soldiers from Michigan decided to deliver Christmas gifts to the locals.

As word of the idea spread, more men got on board— ultimately there were 90 in all. They spent the day before Christmas loading wagons and then taking loads of food (including roasted chickens, turkeys, and sweet potatoes) and supplies to homes throughout the countryside.

We Wish You a Sawadee Pee Mai!

Even if you're not planning a trip around the world this Christmas, these holiday greetings from other countries will come in handy. Try them out on your friends!

Albania: Gezur Krislinjden!

Brazil (Portuguese): Boas Festas!

Ceylon (Singhalese): Subha nath thalak Vewa!

China (Mandarin): Kung His Hsin Nien!

Czech Republic: Prejeme Vam Vesele Vanoce!

Egypt (Arabic): Idah Saidan wa Sanah Jadidah!

England: Merry Christmas!

Finland: Hyvaa joulua!

France: Joyeux Noel!

Germany: Froehliche Weihnachten!

Greece: Kala Christouyenna!

Hawaii: Mele Kalikimaka!

Hungary: Kellemes Karacsonyi!

India (Hindi): Shub Naya Baras!

Indonesia: Selamat Hari Natal!

Iran (Farsi): Cristmas-e-shoma mobarak bashad!

Ireland: Nollaig Shona Dhuit!

Italy: Buone Feste Natalizie!

Japan: Shinnen omedeto, Kurisumasu Omedeto!

Korea: Sung Tan Chuk Ha!

The Netherlands (Dutch): Zalig Kerstfeest!

New Zealand (Maori): Meri Kirihimete!

Nigeria (Yoruba): E ku odun!

Pakistan (Urdu): Naya Saal, Mubarak Ho!

Papua New Guinea: Bikpela hamamas blong dispela Krismas!

Philippines (Tagalog): Maligayamg Pasko!

Poland: Boze Narodzenie!

Russia: Pozdrevlyayu s prazdnikom!

Samoa: La Maunia Le Kilisimasi!

South Africa (Afrikaans): Gesëende Kersfees!

Spain: Feliz Navidad!

Sweden: God Jul!

Thailand: Sawadee Pee Mai!

Turkey: Noeliniz Ve Yeni!

Vietnam: Chung Mung Giang Sinh!

Faux Tannenbaum, Faux Tannenbaum

Here's how the artificial Christmas tree got its start.

Nineteenth-century Germans loved to decorate their homes with freshly cut fir trees (tannenbaum) at Christmas. But that tradition nearly contributed to a national catastrophe: by 1845, deforestation was such a problem that laws limited each family to one Christmas tree per year. Finally, some resourceful German craftsmen solved the problem . . . with sticks and goose feathers.

Trim That Goose

The origin of the first artificial Christmas tree is unknown, but by the 1850s, artisans all over Germany were cranking out small "goose feather" trees. Using sticks and wires for the trunks and branches, the tabletop trees used batches of goose feathers for pine needles. And to add a touch of realism, the artists dyed the feathers green and trimmed the tips of the branches with real berries.

Germans took to the portable feather trees like Santa

takes to cookies, but artificial trees didn't gain a foothold in the American market until Sears Roebuck featured a feather tree in its 1913 catalog. That artificial tree was an instant success. Then in 1933, the Addis Brush Company invented the "Brush Tree," using the same manufacturing process it employed for its toilet brushes. Addis stopped using feathers for needles and instead used animal hair, usually pig bristles, dyed green.

In One Year, Out the Next

In 1950 Addis came up with another innovation: the "Silver Pine." Made of aluminum, it had a revolving light that turned the tree pink, yellow, blue, and green. In the 1960s, aluminum trees were a fad, making up about a third of all Christmas tree sales. Nostalgia won out, though, and by 1972, the artificial tree craze had waned. Real trees were once again the fashion.

But people liked the convenience of artificial trees, so sales quickly recovered. New plastics made the trees easier to assemble, more realistic in appearance, and more durable. Plastic trees offered staggered branches, softer needles, and even built-in fiber-optic lights. By the early 1990s, fake trees outnumbered real ones, and today, more than 50 percent of Americans have artificial trees.

Christmas Down Under

*When it's winter in America, it's summertime in Australia.
Here's how the people Down Under celebrate Christmas.*

- More than 40,000 people visit Sydney's Bondi Beach on
  Christmas Day, and aside from the occasional heat wave or
  cyclone, temperatures average 80°F.

- Because it's so hot, the Australian Santa Claus usually
  wears boardies (surf shorts) and thongs (flip-flops) instead
  of a fuzzy, red-and-white suit.

- Folks in Australia don't trim a traditional European pine.
  They prefer to decorate native flowering plants like the
  Christmas bush, Christmas orchid, and Christmas bells.

- Christmas dessert is usually the Aussie favorite: Pavlova.
  This delicious meringue is crunchy on the outside, like
  marshmallow inside, and topped with whipped cream,
  kiwi, and other fresh fruits.

- The queen of England broadcasts her Christmas speech
  every December 25. For five full minutes, most Aussies
  pause and listen to her talk about family, community, and
  tolerance on the radio or tellie.

- Favorite Aussie carols include "Santa's Moving to the South Pole," "Australians, Let Us Barbeque," and "The Australian Twelve Days of Christmas," where you get pressies like "seven emus running" and "a kookaburra in a gum tree."

- During Australia's 19th-century gold rush, people often baked a gold nugget into their Christmas pudding. Today, the tradition continues with trinkets, and legend says that whoever finds the surprise will have good luck in the new year.

- Traditional Christmas stories include new classics like Mem Fox's *Wombat Divine*, about a wombat cast as baby Jesus in a Christmas nativity play, and *Aussie Night Before Christmas* by Yvonne Morrison, which tells the traditional tale with a twist: Santa drives a rusty old truck pulled by eight great 'roos.

*   *   *

The Day After

Boxing Day (December 26) is a big sports day in Australia. In Melbourne, the Australian cricket team and a touring international team participate in the Boxing Day test match. And in Sydney Harbour, the prestigious Sydney to Hobart Yacht Race begins.

If You Spent Christmas
with Dickens

*Have you ever wondered what Christmas
was like in the 19th century?*

The Man Who "Invented" Christmas?

Charles Dickens dominated 19th-century literature in the
United States and Great Britain. His books—like *Oliver
Twist*, *Great Expectations*, and *David Copperfield*—reached a
wider audience than any writer before him and made him a
literary superstar.

He also had a huge impact on British and American
Christmas celebrations. His 1843 novel *A Christmas Carol*
was a huge success, giving the world the most miserly penny-
pincher of all time: Ebeneezer Scrooge. The book also rein-
troduced traditions like caroling, holiday parties, and good
old Christmas cheer to an England where such festivities
were on the decline. In fact, Dickens's name was so inter-
twined with Christmas that, when he died in 1870, a little
girl in London reportedly said to her father, "Mr. Dickens
dead? Then will Father Christmas die too?"

But what might it have been like to actually celebrate the holiday with its "inventor"? If you've ever wondered, here's you chance. Imagine it's 1843, and you've been invited to spend Christmas in London with the Dickens family.

#1 Devonshire Terrace

The evening would begin with a ride in a horse-drawn cab that would deliver you to the Dickens residence at #1 Devonshire Terrace near London's Regent's Park. You would be greeted by Charles Dickens and his wife Catherine (very pregnant with the fifth of their 10 children).

The Dickens home was always lavishly decorated for the holidays. Holly and ivy draped every table and encircled every chair leg. The family's dazzling Christmas tree was set up in the middle of a great round table and lit by tiny hand-dipped tapers. Its branches were heavy with marzipan candy, gingerbread men, paper fans, cotton-batting Santas, garlands of

cranberries, and strings of paper flowers. A Christmas angel was the family's treasured tree-topper.

Gifts Galore

One of Dickens's favorite traditions was shopping for his family and friends. In 1843 gifts for the kids in his family included wind-up dancing bears, penny whistles, pull toys, stuffed animals, and tiny wax baby dolls in nutshell cradles. Women received embroidered handkerchiefs, fans, or tea balls, and the men got cigar cases or eyeglass cleaner in embroidered pouches.

Another Smoking Bishop, If You Please

Dinner was a sumptuous meal of oysters, roasted chestnuts, turkey, goose, brawn (a jellied meat), and fresh and dried fruits . . . all washed down with steaming mugs of "smoking bishop"—a hot punch made from fruit juice and wine.

Happy Families

After dinner, the company retired to the salon, where guests might dance with Dickens's five-year-old daughter Mary Angela to the fiddle tune "Sir Roger de Coverly," a popular song about a fictional country gentleman. Then eldest son, Charles Culliford Boz Dickens (age six), might talk visitors into a game of Blindman's Buff. Or Charles Dickens might organize a hand of Happy Families. This card game is played with a deck of 44 cards comprised of 11 "families" of a mother, father, son, and daughter with names like Bun the Baker, Pots the Painter, and Bung the Brewer. The goal is to collect the most complete sets of families.

Dickens the Magician

The highlight of the evening, though, would probably be a conjuring act by Dickens himself. The favorite trick? He tossed eggs, flour, and other ingredients for plum pudding into a man's hat. With a wave of his hand, the raw ingredients reappeared boiled, steaming, and ready to eat. For an encore, Dickens changed a pocket handkerchief into comfits (sugar-coated candy made of fruit or nuts), or a box full of bran into a live guinea pig.

*　　　*　　　*

If You Worked for Scrooge, However . . .

- You might live in a single room with 8 to 10 people. Or you might just live on the streets of London.

- You would work six days a week, 12 hours a day, with only Sundays, May Day, and Christmas off.

- If you saved your pennies, you might splurge on a small Christmas goose. It would be have to be roasted by the neighborhood baker, though, because most poor people didn't have ovens.

It's a Wrap

Great moments in the history of gift wrap.

AD 105

The Chinese invented paper and shortly after began using it to wrap gifts. But the emperors fiercely guarded the recipe to make paper, putting to death anyone who tried to steal it. This put a damper on using paper to wrap gifts for the next 1,800 years.

1840

Queen Victoria married Prince Albert from Germany, and the couple popularized celebrating Christmas. (The queen had loved the holiday since childhood, and Albert brought many of Germany's Christmas traditions with him to England.) Wrapping and giving gifts became the rage—for the rich. Most gifts were wrapped simply in green, red, or white tissue paper, but adventurous wrappers used sheets of wallpaper.

1843

After the introduction of the printed Christmas card in 1843, wrapping presents elaborately became popular. Christmas papers started to have intricate design motifs, were lavishly trimmed with lace and ribbon, and often matched a Christmas card. Dominant images: cherubs, robins, angels, holly leaves, and Santa Claus.

1890

The flexography printing process was patented in England, allowing printers to mass-produce decorated, foldable paper for the first time.

1903

Massachusetts-based Hy-Sil Manufacturing Inc., founded by Eli Hyman and Morris Silverman, became America's first gift-wrap company.

1917

The Hall Brothers of Kansas City, Missouri, inadvertently cornered the Christmas wrapping paper market in the United States. Primarily a card manufacturer, the Hall Brothers also sold the usual green, red, and white tissue paper. When the company's retail store ran out of tissue, the Halls had sheets of decorative envelope liners shipped from a manufacturing plant and put them on sale for 10 cents each. The decorative paper sold out quickly. The next year, the Halls sold the sheets three for a quarter . . . and again they sold out.

From then on, the Hall Brothers printed their own line of Christmas wrapping paper, and gift-wrap sales soon were better than those of their greeting card department. The company continues to dominate the greeting card and gift-wrap industry under the corporate name it adopted in the 1930s—Hallmark.

1920s

Because adhesive tape hadn't been invented yet, printers provided circular cutouts of sticky paper with packets of wrapping paper. This freed the gift wrapper from having to use balls of string, sealing wax, and straight pins to hold packages together. Preprinted gift tags became popular, too.

1930s

Decorative patterns on gift-wrap became more stylized, reflecting the popularity of Art Deco. Dominant images: candles, ice-skaters, snowflakes, and Christmas trees.

1930

Minnesota-based 3M invented adhesive "Scotch" tape. (Millions applauded.)

1932

A dispenser with a cutting blade was invented to hold the roll of adhesive tape. (Millions cheered.)

1944

Many luxuries in America were rationed during World War II, but not wrapping paper. Uncle Sam decided that gaily printed wrapping paper would lift the spirits of war-weary Americans. (It did. Sales increased.)

1950s

A nostalgia boom for the "good ol' days" turned the design motifs on wrapping paper back to the realism of the early 20th century. Holly leaves, birds, and other nature images were popular.

1970s

Advertising tie-ins to popular cartoon and movie characters popped up on Christmas paper.

1980s

The decorative gift bag, made of finely printed paper or plastic, was introduced. Bonus innovation: stick-on bows and pre-tied cascade ribbons for the marginally competent wrapper.

*   *   *

"I wish we could put up some of the Christmas spirit in jars and open a jar of it every month."

—*Harlan Miller*

Ghost of Christmas Future

Today, it's iPhones and Wiis, but check out the techie toys people will be clamoring for in the not-so-distant future.

Domestic Robot

Although the technology is still in the works, robotics expert Gordon Wyeth of the University of Queensland, Australia, says that within the next decade or so, domestic robots will be the new must-have for the family home. They will be walking, talking robots ready to cook dinner, vacuum the living room, or mow the backyard. Wyeth's prototype is a completely autonomous humanoid robot named GuRoo, who stands about four feet tall and weighs 100 pounds. Wyeth (and GuRoo) are also regular competitors in the annual International RoboCup World Cup Soccer Games—"the world's most renowned intelligent robotics competition."

Skycar

Moller International, a California-based technology company, has developed the world's first feasible and affordable personal vertical takeoff and landing (VTOL) vehicle—which looks a lot like George Jetson's car in the TV show. The M400 Skycar can cruise comfortably at 275 mph (maximum speed is 375 mph) and achieve up to 20 miles per gallon on clean-burning, ethanol fuel. Moller International plans to deliver Skycars to the U.S. military in 2010.

Smart Clothing

Imagine this: You're on a hike in the Alps and start climbing a steep hill. As you start to tire, your boots inform you that you've just burned half the calories you consumed at Christmas dinner. Gloating a little, you power on . . . and trip, hitting your head on a rock. You're out as cold as last night's turkey. Maybe you weren't smart enough to go hiking with a buddy, but at least you wore your Smart T-shirt—and it has already called the paramedics.

That's Smart Clothing, one of the innovations being developed by scientists at Derby University, England. The high-performance, computerized sportswear can monitor bodily functions, report in, and call for help when necessary. And in case you need even more advance warning, researchers at Australia's University of Wollongong are busy working on clothing that will groan when you move or stretch in ways that could injure you.

*   *   *

First state to make Christmas a holiday: Alabama in 1836.

I Want a Schreckengost!

*Like Santa Claus, Viktor Schreckengost worked hard
all year, designing toys for children of all ages.*

It's safe to say that between 1939 and 1970 most American
kids wanted to find a Viktor Schreckengost bicycle under
their Christmas tree. As the head designer for the Murray
Ohio bicycle company, his products were sleek and supersonic-
looking. In 1939 his Mercury bicycle was introduced at the
New York World's Fair and became an instant hit. It was
streamlined and looked like a chrome motorcycle with
ultracool fenders and a rocket-shaped light.

In 1940 Schreckengost introduced the Pursuit Pedal
Plane—a kid's pedal car that looked like an airplane. That
joined the ranks of his pedal fire trucks, racecars, and atomic
missiles. And in 1969 the Mach II banana seat bike, which
enabled kids to shift their weight and do wheelies without
falling off, was at the top of many Christmas lists.

Little Geppetto

Viktor Schreckengost got his start as a toymaker. Encouraged by his father and uncles, who were commercial potters in Sebring, Ohio, Schreckengost crafted toy soldiers and animals out of scraps of clay and then glazed them with melted crayons. His father held weekly sculpture contests among young Viktor and his five siblings to inspire the kids to keep working.

Schreckengost soon moved beyond clay and built a plywood airplane (with a 10-foot wingspan) from piano crates. He used a wound-up inner tube to power the propeller and talked a friend into test-flying it off the third-story fire escape at their elementary school. The plane smashed to bits just moments after launch, but luckily the friend wasn't injured.

The Million-Idea Man

After graduating from the Cleveland School of the Arts in 1929, Schreckengost went to work as a designer for Murray Ohio. While there, his innovations included the first inexpensive children's pedal cars, which were built from a single piece of metal. He also halved the cost of making a bicycle by automating the welding. In the 40 years that Schreckengost designed for Murray Ohio, the company sold more than 50 million of his bicycles, making it the largest bicycle manufacturer in the world.

Schreckengost didn't focus only on Murray Ohio; he worked for other places, too. He created the Industrial

Design division at the Cleveland Institute of Art and was on its faculty from 1933 to 2008. He designed the Spaceliner bicycle for Sears and china for Limoges. And he created an Art Deco ceramic bowl for Eleanor Roosevelt called "the Jazz Bowl." It sold at an auction in 2004 for $250,000.

"Schreckengost," said one reporter, "made, quite literally, the stuff of life." He designed all the things found in most kitchens, living rooms, backyards, and garages worldwide. The list includes everything from furniture to military radar systems, printing presses to stoves, rider lawn mowers to coffins, and calendars, electric fans, lenses, ball gowns, artificial limbs, flashlights, and baby walkers. With all of those designs, Schreckengost rightly earned the title of the "American da Vinci."

Gone But Not Forgotten

In 2006 Schreckengost received the National Medal of Arts, the highest cultural award in the United States. He died in 2008 at the age of 101, but the Viktor Schreckengost legacy lives on. Nearly 100 million of his bicycles have been sold. His steel lawn chair still graces millions of American backyards, and his idea of putting the cab of a truck over its engine is used in almost every city bus today.

Bring Us Some Figgy Pudding

Some people call it steamed pudding or Christmas pudding, but it's all the dessert that gets its own verse in "We Wish You a Merry Christmas." In case you were wondering where it came from or you wanted to whip up a batch for your next holiday party, we tracked down the details.

"Un-fit for God-fearing People"?

More like a cake than a pudding, figgy pudding has a long (and steamy) reputation. In the mid-1600s, the Puritans in England actually banned it, and political leader Oliver Cromwell called it a "lewd custom . . . unfit for God-fearing people." (The proper Puritans believed that the fruit spices and alcohol in the pudding inflamed passions.) The Quakers also condemned it as "the invention of the scarlet whore of Babylon."

But the English held on to the tradition, and slowly it made its way to the New World, complete with its own rituals and superstitions.

- Everyone in the house should help make the pudding, and as they stir, they should make a wish.

- Some families hide a small toy or trinket in the batter. The person who finds it will have good luck.

Here's a recipe that will make two figgy puddings—one for you and one for a friend.

Ingredients

- 1 cup dried figs
- 1 cup breadcrumbs
- 1 cup suet (beef fat) (You can also use butter or shortening.)
- 1 cup sultanas
- 1 cup raisins
- 1 cup currants
- 1 cup brown sugar
- ¼ cup flaked almonds
- ¼ cup plain flour
- ½ cup mixed peel (orange, lemon)
- 2 tsp. mixed spice (cinnamon, ginger, nutmeg)
- ¼ pint rum or brandy
- 4 large eggs (beaten)
- 1 pinch salt
- milk (if necessary)

Two Weeks Before Christmas

- Put the figs in a saucepan, add water, and bring to a boil. Lower the heat and continue cooking until the figs are soft and can be easily mashed with a wooden spoon.

- Mix everything together in a large bowl. If the mix is too dry, add a little milk.

- Pack the mix into a greased bundt or kugel pan and cover

with greaseproof paper. The pudding will expand while cooking, so if the pan is filled to the top, make a pleat in the paper to allow for the expansion. Tie it down tightly with string, and make a loop from one side to the other to act as a handle.

- Put the pan on a trivet in a covered stockpot with enough water to come halfway up the side; bring it to a boil.
- Reduce the heat and simmer for two hours; add more water as necessary. Once it has cooled, wrap it up in plastic film, and stow it in the fridge.

On Christmas Day

- Cook the same way for another two hours.
- Bring it to the table covered with flaming brandy.
- Serve with cream or brandy butter.

*   *   *

Shop 'Til You Drop

Most people (and certainly the TV media) think that "Black Friday," the day after Thanksgiving, is the busiest shopping day of the year. Not so—it's usually fourth or fifth. The Saturday before Christmas is almost always the busiest.

The Radio City Music Hall Christmas Spectacular

More than a million people flock to New York's Radio City Music Hall every year just to catch this show.

When "The Radio City Music Hall Christmas Spectacular" premiered in 1933, it was just filler meant to be performed between movie screenings at the brand-new Radio City Music Hall. Moviegoers who came to watch *Lady for a Day* or *42nd Street* were treated to 36 Rockettes tapping and dancing with dazzling precision. But it wasn't long before the entr'acte became more popular than the main event.

Big Is Better

Since that time, the annual production has evolved into a 90-minute spectacle, and the high-kicking Rockettes remain its centerpiece. The dancers perform eight precision tap numbers that include audience favorites like "The March of the Tin Soldiers," in which they dance in pants that are so starched they can stand on their own. A cast of more than

100 singers and dancers, including Santa Claus, supports the show.

But *Bigger* Is Fantastic!

Nothing is too big for the Radio City Music Hall stage, which at 100 feet wide by 60 feet high is twice as big as most Broadway stages. In fact, it's the largest indoor theater in the world. Look what happens on it during the show:

- Crew members roll in a real ice rink for the "Christmas in New York" scene.

- During the "Music Hall Menagerie," two donkeys, three camels, five sheep, and a horse make cameo appearances.

- Every one of the show's 140 cast members is onstage in a Santa costume during the "Here Comes Santa Claus" number (which claims to explain how Santa can actually deliver gifts to every boy and girl in the world all in one night).

- 2,500 pounds of fake snow drops onto the stage.

- For the Radio City Music Hall's 75th anniversary, audiences were given 3-D glasses and treated to a 3-D bus ride through New York City—with the Rockettes as tour guides, of course!

To read more about the Rockettes,
turn to page 28.

Pop Christmas Quiz

Match the singer with his or her holiday hit. (Answers are on page 176.)

1. John Lennon   **a.** "My Only Wish (This Year)"

2. Joni Mitchell   **b.** "Merry Christmas, Baby"

3. Ringo Starr   **c.** "Santa Baby"

4. Mariah Carey   **d.** "River"

5. Madonna   **e.** "I Wish Everyday Could Be Like Christmas"

6. Paul McCartney   **f.** "Happy Xmas (War is Over)"

7. Garth Brooks   **g.** "Wonderful Christmastime"

8. Britney Spears   **h.** "Santa Looked A Lot Like Daddy"

9. Bruce Springsteen   **i.** "All I Want for Christmas is You"

10. Bon Jovi   **j.** "I Wanna Be Santa Claus"

*   *   *

Bonus Round!

What girl group released "8 Days of Christmas" in 2001?

a. Wilson Phillips   **c.** Dixie Chicks

b. Destiny's Child   **d.** Pussycat Dolls

Happy Hogmanay

Here's another Christmastime tradition from another part of the world. This time: Scotland.

The tradition of celebrating Christmas with gifts and parties was almost nonexistent in Scotland for nearly 400 years. Puritanical Protestants dominated Scottish religious life from the end of the 17th century to as late as the 1970s, and since they felt Christmas was a Catholic holiday, they didn't want to celebrate it. So while the rest of the Western world trimmed trees and hung stockings, the Scots worked through Christmas and put all of their holiday cheer into celebrating the last day of the year: a holiday they called Hogmanay.

The word comes either from the northern French term *hoguinane*, meaning "New Year's gift," or the Scottish Gaelic words *og-mhadainn*, meaning "first morning." But no matter its origin, all Scots agree on its meaning—party hearty! Festivities begin on New Year's Eve and go well into the wee hours of Ne'er Day (New Year's Day). Celebrations include feasts, fireworks . . . and a few unique customs.

A Clean Start

On December 31, homes get a thorough "redding," or cleaning. Not only is the house scoured from top to bottom, but also all debts should be paid before midnight. Ashes from the day's last fire are swept up and read like tea leaves to divine what good fortune the coming year will bring.

First Footing

At the stroke of midnight, Scots link hands with family and friends and sing a rousing chorus of Robert Burns's "Auld Lang Syne." (*More about that song on page 111.*) To ensure good luck for the house, the first foot that crosses the threshold after midnight should belong to a tall, dark man bringing gifts of coal, shortbread, salt, black bun (fruitcake), and whiskey. This is probably a throwback to the 9th century, when Vikings raided Scotland and blond visitors meant big trouble. The gifts of coal and food make sure that the house stays warm and safe and that the inhabitants never go hungry.

Ne'er Day

Each area of Scotland has its own New Year's Day ritual: The residents of Fife put on a torchlight procession. And in Stonehaven on Scotland's east coast, the ancient Fireballs ceremony involves 60 locals marching through town swinging flaming spheres above their heads.

Letters to Santa

These are actual letters written with love and handled with care.

Dear Santa,

I only want one little thing for Christmas this year. Please bring me an elf. I promise not to let the dog get it.

—Cailey

Dear Santa,

Don't use the chimney this year. Dad put a wall there. Use the front door instead.

—Lawson

Dear Santa,

This year could I please have a girl rat? It would be nice for it to have been hand-raised butt that's up to you.

—Dash

Dear Santa,

What list am I on, the naughty or nice list? If I'm on the naughty, what could I do to get off?

—Ashley

The Gingerbread
White House

Not all Christmas traditions go back hundreds of years.

White House chefs have been making gingerbread houses every Christmas since the 1950s. But it wasn't until 1979, when First Lady Rosalyn Carter hired Roland Mesnier to serve as head pastry chef, that the tradition became an event. Mesnier had been cooking since his teens, when his mother got him an apprenticeship at a bakery near their home in eastern France. There, he learned to love making deserts, especially fresh desserts. So it was no surprise that when he started working at the White House, he vowed to make everything he served on site. From the ice cream to the cookies to the state dinners, Mesnier and his staff made everything there.

Themed Cooking

He made the gingerbread, too. From that first year, Mesnier created gingerbread houses for the presidents and first families. The houses started out simple: He made an edible replica of the White House for the Carters. For the Reagans, he added a chimney and sidewalk made from the president's favorite treat, jellybeans. But with new administrations came more elaborate structures that evolved from single houses with edible chairs and furniture to whole villages with edible people and pets. In 1995 Mesnier spent five months re-creating Hilary Clinton's family home in Park Ridge, Illinois, complete with tiny stuffed stockings and sugarplums.

In 2003 the theme was "A Season of Stories," and Laura Bush (an ex-librarian) asked Mesnier to build a replica of Willy Wonka's factory from Roald Dahl's book, *Charlie and the Chocolate Factory*. It took more than six months, 80 pounds of chocolate, and 10 pounds each of lollipops and bubblegum to build the masterpiece. Chocolate gushed from the tops of the cakes, and all the pipes inside the factory were hollow and made of sugar. That same year, Mesnier also built a gingerbread replica of the White House that was taller than usual because he added 60 marzipan storybook characters to the structure, including *Jack and the Beanstock*, the *Three Little Pigs* and *James and the Giant Peach*. Through an open window, visitors could even see the room from *Goodnight Moon*.

Mesnier retired in 2004, but the gingerbread tradition continues in the White House's East Wing with new head pastry chef, Thaddeus R. DuBois.

For more about gingerbread to turn pages 22 and 108.

Party Puzzlers

Need something to do at your next Christmas party?
See if your guests know the answers to these trivia
questions. (Answers on page 177.)

1. How many times are the Three Wise Men mentioned in the Bible?

    a. 0

    b. 3

    c. 7

2. Who created the first Nativity scene with live animals?

    a. P. T. Barnum

    b. St. Francis of Assisi

    c. Queen Elizabeth I

3. What is Christmas called in France?

    a. Nuit Divin

    b. Noel

    c. L'anniversaire du Christ

4. During the Vietnam War, what song did the U.S. military choose to be the radio signal for the immediate evacuation of Saigon?

    a. "I'll Be Home for Christmas"

    b. "Silent Night"

    c. "White Christmas"

5. Have Yourself a Merry Little Christmas" is from what classic movie?

    a. *Holiday Inn*

    b. *White Christmas*

    c. *Meet Me in St. Louis*

6. If you were a member of the Goose Club in Victorian England, what would that mean?

    a. You raised prize-winning geese for Christmas.

    b. You met with friends at an exclusive club for a Christmas goose dinner.

    c. You put money aside each month in a savings account toward purchasing a Christmas goose.

7. Two *Sesame Street* puppets have the same names as a policeman and a cab driver featured in what Christmas movie?

    a. *It's a Wonderful Life*

    b. *Miracle on 34th Street*

    c. *The Bishop's Wife*

Mr. Christmas?

For this Englishman, Christmas comes
365 times a year . . . or does it?

He Needs a Little Christmas

Imagine waking up every morning to find it's Christmas. You breakfast on mince pies and sherry, and then open your presents. As you watch the Queen's Christmas Message on your tellie, you feast on slices of roast turkey. When you go to sleep that night, you know that tomorrow will bring yet another seasonal celebration. Andy Park has had that kind of day, every day . . . for 15 years.

It all began in July 1993, when the 31-year-old electrician was feeling fed up with life. He decided to do something to shake his chronic boredom, so he decorated his house with Christmas decorations. Suddenly, he felt happy, so he did it again the next day. And the next. And the next.

The Gift That Keeps on Giving

Now Park makes sure there's always a Christmas tree at his home (he's gone through more than 30 artificial ones). Every morning, after a breakfast of mince pies and a glass of sherry, he unwraps the present he bought for himself the day before. (Over the years he's gotten himself some great gifts: a Mercedes, a VCR, movies, suits, and dinner jackets.) Park then goes to work, and when he returns home, he has a holiday feast with champagne and watches a video of the Queen's Christmas speech.

The Bottom Line

Celebrating Christmas every day has its costs. Park claims he has consumed 4,380 turkeys, 87,600 mince pies, 2,190 pints of gravy, 26,280 roast potatoes, 219,000 mushy peas, 4,380 bottles of champagne, 4,380 bottles of sherry, and 5,000 bottles of wine. (All of that has caused Andy Park's weight to balloon to more than 260 pounds.) Add in the cost of lights and decorations ($20,000) and the 21,900 presents he's given to himself in the past 12 years, and his bill comes to about $375,000. But Mr. Christmas, as he's come to be known, feels it's worth it.

In 2006 Park offered the queen the use of his home for broadcasting her Christmas speech. (As her "biggest fan," he does watch her speech every day of the year.) She respectfully declined. Park was disappointed and said, "The queen doesn't know what she's missing. I had the day all worked out: a roast, drinks, crackers, a game of Scrabble, carols, the speech, and then maybe a kiss under the mistletoe."

Mr. Scam Artist?

Not everyone believes Park's celebratory claims, though. In December 2005, MSNBC television host Keith Olbermann talked about Park on his show and mentioned his concerns that Mr. Christmas was a fraud. According to Olbermann, a German news crew stopped by Park's home, wanting to interview him and to photograph his holiday activities. But Park asked for £200 (almost $400) for the interview, and when the crew refused to pay, he sent them home.

Olbermann did a little more investigating and found that other news agencies had trouble pinning Park down, too. His local paper had given up trying to interview him because he always turned away their crews. And according to the *Daily Mail*, who visited him just a few weeks before Olbermann's show, Park was at home eating chicken. (He said it was just a snack while he waited for the turkey to thaw.)

To top it all off, Park's numbers don't always match either. Sometimes Mr. Christmas says he's eaten 4,380 turkeys, but other times, he puts the number at more than 9,000. And he alters the number of brussel sprouts he's eaten, too, offering various figures from just over 100,000 to more than a quarter of a million. Given all the inconsistencies and speculation, there's no way for us to be sure that Mr. Christmas actually celebrates the holiday year-round as he says, but we sure do like the idea.

Hardtack Holiday

Pioneers faced many hardships when they moved west, and often they had to do without necessities. But even in the unsettled wilderness, they made sure to celebrate Christmas.

A Christmas Feast by Any Other Name

Members of Captain John C. Fremont's 1848 expedition to explore the West found themselves holed up in the rugged southern Colorado mountains for Christmas. Game was scarce, and fierce winter weather kept the men inside a crude stockade shelter they'd dubbed Camp Desolation. But they were determined to celebrate Christmas, so they improvised. One man recorded the day's menu in his journal:

Bill of Fare

Camp Desolation, December 25, 1848

Soup: Mule Tail

Meats: Mule Steak, Fried Mule, Mule Chops, Boiled Mule, Stewed Mule, Scrambled Mule, Shirred Mule, French-Fried Mule, Minced Mule, Damned Mule, Mule on Toast (without the toast), Short Ribs of Mule with Apple Sauce (without the apple sauce).

Beverages: Snow, Snow Water, Water

He concluded the entry by writing: "It really makes no difference how our meat was cooked. It was the same old mule."

Lewis and Clark's Christmas

In 1805 during their second winter on the trail, Meriwether Lewis, William Clark, their expedition, and some Native guests spent a damp Christmas at Fort Clatsop in Oregon. Their uniforms were shredded and soggy, they'd run out of liquor, and they barely had enough food. But still they made merry. On Christmas morning, the men fired their guns and "feasted" on spoiled fish, boiled elk, and wild roots. They even exchanged gifts: the men who smoked divided up the tobacco, and the ones who didn't got handkerchiefs as presents.

See Them Tumbling Down

In the early 1800s, the custom of the decorating Christmas tree made its way across the Great Plains with migrating German settlers. But in some places, there were no evergreens (or any trees, for that matter). So what did the resourceful pioneers decorate? Tumbleweeds.

Virtual Christmas

Life out West could be bleak for pioneers. Many lived in sod houses, and thin layers of dust—blown in from the prairie or desert—covered everything inside. But still, the settlers celebrated the Christmas holidays. Stories of the day describe scenes like this: Instead of an evergreen, a sapling decorated with scraps of paper and pieces of mattress batting for "snow" stood by a smoking fire pit. On Christmas morning, a teenage boy might find a new rifle under the tree, his father got a badly needed saddle, and his mother oohed and ahed over a crisp gingham dress. But the Christmas gifts weren't real—they were illustrations cut out of a catalog. This practice was common among poor and isolated homesteaders from New Mexico to Montana during the 19th century, who refused to let reality destroy their celebration.

Little Christmas on the Prairie

Laura Ingalls Wilder, author of *The Little House on the Prairie*, celebrated some of her early Christmases in rural Kansas. Her family had little to spare for the holidays, but Wilder wrote in her books that her "Ma" spent the day cooking "rye'n'injun bread" (cornbread made with honey and rye instead of sugar and flour), vinegar pies, and Swedish crackers (hardtack crispy crackers). And on Christmas Day, Wilder was delighted to find in her stocking a shiny new tin cup, a peppermint candy, a heart-shaped cake, and a brand new penny.

Merry Christmas: From Irving, Felix, and Mel Part 2

We conclude our list of the top Christmas carols written by Jewish composers. (Turn to page 101 for the first part of the story.)

#10: "Rudolph the Red-Nosed Reindeer"
#14: "Rockin' Around the Christmas Tree"
#17: "A Holly Jolly Christmas"

The only songwriter to score a triple on this list is Johnny Marks, who wrote all three of these songs and charted Top 10 hits in three decades: the 1940s, 50s, and 60s.

#11: "It's the Most Wonderful Time of the Year"

Before moving to Los Angeles in 1946, George Wyle was a piano player in the "Borscht Belt," a resort area in New York's Catskill Mountains where entertainers like Milton Berle and Sid Caesar honed their skills. For the next 20 years, Wyle worked as a television show conductor for Jerry Lewis, Dinah Shore, Doris Day, and Andy Williams, for whom he wrote "It's the Most Wonderful Time of the Year" in 1964. It's been a staple on holiday albums ever since. (Wyle also wrote the theme song for *Gilligan's Island*.)

#12: "I'll Be Home for Christmas"

Composer Walter Kent and lyricists Buck Ram and Kim Gannon wrote this for Bing Crosby in 1943, giving him his second consecutive number-one Christmas hit. ("White Christmas" in 1942 was the first.)

#13: "Silver Bells"

Jay Livingston (Jacob Harold Levison) and Ray Evans (who was Jewish, though how he got the Welsh last name is a mystery) penned this song in 1951 for the Bob Hope movie *The Lemon Drop Kid*. Evans later wrote that he was inspired by the sound of the Salvation Army bell ringers on the city street. Evans and Livingston collaborated on three other Oscar-winning songs ("Buttons and Bows," "Mona Lisa," and "Que Sera, Sera") and wrote the theme music for the TV shows *Bonanza* and *Mr. Ed*.

#22: "(There's No Place Like) Home for the Holidays"

Al Stillman teamed with Bob Allen on this 1954 hit for Perry Como. They also had hits for Johnny Mathis ("Chances Are") and the Four Lads ("Moments to Remember").

Happy Merry Birthday

*In 1891 Robert Louis Stevenson—author of the classic
stories* Treasure Island *and* Dr. Jekyll and Mr.
Hyde*—came up with the best present ever.*

While living in Samoa in the late 19th century, Robert Louis Stevenson befriended Annie Ide, the 14-year-old daughter of the island's governor, Henry Ide. Annie complained to Stevenson that she felt cheated because her birthday fell on Christmas Day, which meant she received presents only once a year. In response, Stevenson promptly sat down and wrote this document:

I, Robert Louis Stevenson . . . a British subject, being in sound mind, and pretty well, I thank you, in body; In consideration that Miss Annie H. Ide . . . was born, out of all reason, upon Christmas Day, and is, therefore, out of all justice, denied the consolation and profit of a proper birthday;

And considering that I, the said Robert Louis Stevenson, have attained the age when we never mention it, and that I have now no further use for a birthday of any description . . . I have transferred, and do hereby transfer, to the said Annie

H. Ide, all and whole of my rights and privileges in the 13th day of November, formerly my birthday, now, hereby and henceforth, the birthday of the said Annie H. Ide, to have, hold, exercise, and enjoy the same in the customary manner, by the sporting of fine raiment, eating of rich meats, and receipt of gifts, compliments, and copies of verse, according to the manner of our ancestors;

And I direct the said Annie H. Ide to add to the said name of Annie H. Ide the name of Louisa [to match Stevenson's "Louis"]—at least in private—and I charge her to use my said birthday with moderation and humanity . . . the said birthday not being so young as it once was and having carried me in a very satisfactory manner since I can remember;

And in case the said Annie H. Ide shall neglect or contravene either of the above conditions, I hereby revoke the donation and transfer my rights in the said birthday to the President of the United States of America for the time being.

More Secret Santas

Ordinary people are spreading good will across the country.

Kansas

Lynn Hinkle of Kansas City started her own annual Secret Santa project in 2006. She took her three teenage sons and two nieces to a hotel and had them stuff the maids' carts with $20 and $50 bills.

Massachusetts

On December 16, 2006, a 37-year-old man from Westborough, Massachusetts, discovered a box with a white bow sitting on the front seat of his parked car. A note accompanying the box said, "Merry Christmas. Thank you for leaving your car door unlocked. Instead of stealing your car I gave you a present. Hopefully this will land in the hands of someone you love, for my love is gone now." What was inside the box? A $15,000 diamond ring.

Missouri

In 1996 Terry Franz, a used-car dealer in Kansas City,

decided to give away some cars to people who couldn't afford them. He originally meant the gesture as a promotional gimmick to publicize his dealership, but the gesture was so meaningful to Franz that he started an organization called Cars 4 Christmas. Today, Franz is no longer a car dealer and instead devotes much of his time to getting people to donate used cars, hiring mechanics to fix them up, and finding local charities to distribute them to deserving recipients. When asked what happened to his used-car lot, Franz replied, "I do better at giving cars away than selling them, I guess."

Virginia

Mr. K admits that it all began as a joke. After overindulging with a little holiday punch in 1986, he and his friends decided to go water-skiing on the Potomac River on Christmas Eve dressed like Santa and his elves. That was more than 20 years ago, and the "joke" has now become an annual event.

Every year at 1:00 p.m. on Christmas Eve, Mr. K (whose identity has never been revealed) departs Columbia Island Marina near the Pentagon with an entourage of 35 that includes a knee-boarding reindeer, flying elves, a jet-skiing Grinch, and Frosty the Snowman in a dinghy. They all use code names like Mr. K (as in Kris Kringle) and show up faithfully no matter how bad the weather—one year, when the Potomac was frozen over, an icebreaker boat forged a path through the pack ice so Santa would not disappoint his fans. The entire water-skiing parade takes about 18 minutes, and there are no logos, no banners, no sponsors—just pure, freezing fun.

New York

On December 25, 1996, this letter was printed in the *New York Times*:

To the Editor:

I am a kindergarten teacher at P.S. 181 in the Springfield Gardens section of Queens. My 26 students wrote letters to Santa Claus. I sent him the letters in care of the General Post Office in Manhattan. In response I received a Christmas card from Santa for my children and a personal note. He said that he was very busy this year and asked if I could purchase gifts for my children for him. Enclosed were seven $100 gift certificates to Macy's!

I do not know who sent this wonderful gift to my children. The card was signed "Santa Claus." There was no return address. The postmark on the envelope said "Westchester." So, to Santa Claus in Westchester, thank you for making this a memorable holiday for me and my students.

—Carol Samnick, Plainview, Long Island

Eggnog

*At 400 years old, eggnog has a long history
as America's favorite holiday drink.*

I n the days before iceboxes and refrigerators, eggs and milk
spoiled easily. But mixing them with alcohol was one way
to extend their shelf life. During the Renaissance, the English
drank something called "posset," a hot concoction made
from eggs, milk, and ale that was more of a custard than a
drink. Then came the cold drink, eggnog, which means "egg
in a cup." (In taverns, the wooden cup used to serve nog,
Old English slang for ale, was called a "noggin.")

Take One Eggnog and Call Me in the Morning

One of the oldest recipes for eggnog comes from an English
woman named Elinor Fettiplace. In 1604 she recommended
a drink made of egg yolk, milk, and a brandylike liquor
called aqua vitae as medicine for "a great cold." And eggnog,
made with brandy and Madeira wine, was sometimes used as
a cure for a hangover. Add a few aromatic spices like nutmeg,
and it was a tasty beverage.

Versions of eggnog quickly became popular among all of the aristocracies of Europe, the only people who could afford eggs and milk on a regular basis. They mixed their drinks with Madeira, brandy, wine, or sherry. But it was in colonial America that eggnog caught on with everyday people.

A Rum Tale

According to Captain John Smith, the Jamestown colonists started making eggnog shortly after their arrival in 1607. Since brandy was highly taxed and expensive, they switched to rum, which at the time was cheaper than beer.

By the end of the Revolutionary War, eggnog as we know it was a staple at holiday parties. An English tourist aptly summed up the American predilection for eggnog in 1866: "Christmas is not properly observed unless you brew egg nogg for all comers. Everybody calls on everybody else; and each call is celebrated by a solemn egg-nogging. It is made cold and is drunk cold and is to be commended."

First in War, First in Peace, First in Nog

George Washington was renowned for his Christmas parties and for his personal eggnog recipe:

1 quart cream	½ pint rye whiskey
1 quart milk	¼ pint rum
1 dozen eggs	¼ pint sherry
1 pint brandy	

Santa Calling

William Joyce has authored and illustrated many best-selling books, but it was his Christmas tale Santa Calls *that became one of his most personal successes.*

North Pole Post

The idea for *Santa Calls* was inspired by Joyce's nephews, who in the late 1980s received elaborate letters from Santa Claus every Christmas Eve. Each letter came in an illustrated envelope postmarked "North Pole Post" or "Elf Express" and described the events of the previous year at Santa's Workshop. (Interestingly, the writing and Art Deco-like illustrations in these letters resembled Joyce's own illustrations and writing

style.) There were tales about Santa's trip to the moon, the year it was so cold that all of the elves froze, and how much Santa's pet polar bear liked elf juggling.

One year, though, Santa didn't send a letter, and the nephews were devastated. The following Christmas, they received especially long letters telling them of the harrowing experience Santa's elf Londo had endured while trying to deliver the previous year's correspondence. It was an elaborate story of polar bears, penguins, and adventure. And that letter got William Joyce thinking about what might happen if Santa really were in trouble. He imagined Santa sending a distress call to three kids in Abilene, Texas, in the form of a large crate that contained a magical flying machine and a mysterious note asking for help.

What a Story!

It took two years for Joyce to write and illustrate *Santa Calls*, but on its publication in 1993, the book became an award-winning success. In 1994 and 1995, Saks Fifth Avenue asked Joyce to design windows for its store based on scenes from the book. Joyce also designed Santa ornaments and gifts. And the National Center for Children's Illustrated Literature in Abilene, Texas, commissioned a 12-foot-tall sculpture to commemorate the story.

Big Kids Have More Fun

William Joyce has always had a soft spot for Christmas . . . all holidays, actually. Every Fourth of July, he stages the Big Fourth of July Blow-up at his home in Shreveport, Louisiana, where he and his family and friends set out thousands of red, white, and blue plastic figurines of army men, ballerinas, dinosaurs, and animals—and blow them up with firecrackers. Joyce also takes off the month of October to decorate for

Halloween—it's not just carved pumpkins and hanging spiderwebs, either. Joyce paints his entire living room with Halloween murals. And he pulls out more than 100 skeletons from his closet and places them in ghastly arrangements around the house.

As Christmas approaches, he replaces the ghoulies and ghosties on the living room walls with falling snowflakes. A Christmas tree is set in every bedroom, and five fully decorated trees fill the living room, creating an indoor forest. As Joyce says in his book *The World of William Joyce Scrapbook*, "Though we live in the South, where it's kind of hot, we try to have a cool Yule."

* * *

Christmas Quotables

"Christmas is not a time nor a season, but a state of mind. To cherish peace and goodwill, to be plenteous in mercy, is to have the real spirit of Christmas."

—Calvin Coolidge

"The only real blind person at Christmastime is he who has not Christmas in his heart."

—Helen Keller

Making Merchandise Merry

You may have a great idea, but marketing makes it possible to get your product on store shelves in time for Christmas.

Just Tinker with It

Charles Pajeau, an Evanston, Illinois, stoneworker, conceived of Tinker Toys in 1913 after observing some kids playing with pencils, sticks, and empty spools of thread. He designed the toy in his garage and brought the finished product—packed in its famous canister—to the 1914 American International Toy Fair in New York City, but the buyers weren't interested. So Pajeau waited until Christmas and then dressed some "little people" in elf costumes and paid them to play with Tinker Toys in the windows of Chicago's Marshall Field's department store. That did the trick—a year later, he'd sold more than a million sets.

The Singing Sandwich

In 2005 Great Britain's largest retailer, Tesco, introduced a new product for Christmas: the Musical Sandwich. Shoppers who purchased one at a Tesco store would get a singing surprise when they opened the container. Moving the lid activated a device that played a Christmas carol, just like a musical greeting card. Initially, customers found the sandwich (sliced turkey with cranberry sauce) to be pretty good, but the music (a medley of "Jingle Bells," "Santa Claus Is Coming to Town," and "We Wish You a Merry Christmas") to be very annoying. It was a hit that first year, but then fizzled.

Hitler Vino

Winegrower Alessandro Lunardelli discovered his own niche Christmas market in 1995 when he began selling bottles of wine named after famous dictators and leaders. The Benito Mussolini and Napoleon labels did fairly well, but his "Führerwein" won him (infamous) fame and fortune. The public was so outraged at seeing Adolf Hitler's face on the wine bottles that two major cities—Brussels and Berlin— tried to have it banned. This, of course, was the perfect publicity. Today, Lunardelli's northern Italian vineyard sells 100,000 bottles of wine a year. At 8 euros (about $12.50) a bottle and continuing to feature labels of controversial historical figures (like Hitler, Joseph Stalin, and Che Guevara), the wine has made Lunardelli a very rich man.

That's a Wrap

When it comes to promotion, few entrepreneurs can match Christopher Radko, whose sparkling glass Christmas ornaments have hung on the White House tree under Republican and Democratic presidents as well as in the homes of celebrities like Robert Redford, Oprah Winfrey, and Elton John. Radko now lords over a Christmas ornament empire worth $50 million. More than 3,000 artists work for him in Europe and the United States. They make all of the ornaments by hand, and each one takes seven days to complete.

But he wasn't always so successful. In the 1980s, Radko was a working actor who accidentally broke all his family's decades-old Christmas ornaments. In an effort to replace them, he went to Poland where he sketched the pieces for a glassblower. He brought the ornaments home, and his friends were so enamored with them that they bought them all. That's when he knew he had a great product.

Getting the word out about the ornaments was going to be hard. Radko's preferred means of promotion? He just gave the ornaments away: $50,000 worth of mantel decorations went to the Clinton White House alone.

In 1997 Radko demonstrated another kind of promotional flair: he wrapped a mile of red ribbon around the Kennedy Center in Washington, D.C., making it look like a

 giant Christmas present. "I wanted . . . to be able to see [it] from 50 miles away," Radko said. Next on his agenda: Wrapping the North Pole. No details yet on how he intends to pull that off.

Rewriting the Carols

See if you can decipher the real Christmas carol from the rephrased version below. (Answers are on page 178.)

1. "Listen! The Winged Messengers Harmonize"

2. "Festoon the Corridors with Limbs of *Ilex Aquifolium*"

3. "The Tiny Male Juvenile Timpanist"

4. "Snow Carriage Journey"

5. "Quiet Evening, Sacred Evening"

6. "Strolling Through a Snowy Paradise"

7. "Tree Seeds Barbecuing Atop the Burning Logs"

8. "I'll Experience a Depressing Yuletide Sans Your Presence"

9. "Get Over Here, You True Believers"

10. "Rimey the Frozen Precipitation Being"

11. "We, the Trio of Potentates from the Far East, Exist"

12. "Praise the Lord Refrain"

13. "I Spied My Maternal Unit Sucking Face with St. Nick"

14. "My Sole Request This Yuletide Is the Forward Duo of My Upper Incisors"

15. "A Dozen Solar Risings of Jesus's Birthday"

Holiday Whodunnit

*Or, rather, who really wrote the most famous
Christmas poem of all time?*

It may be the best-known poem in the United States, and one of the few that most Americans can recite from memory. Thanks to Clement Clarke Moore, a biblical scholar from New York City, and his 1823 poem, "A Visit from St. Nicholas" ("The Night Before Christmas"), children still hang their stockings "by the chimney with care" before going to bed on Christmas Eve. Also thanks to the poem, the image of Santa Claus changed from a stern authoritarian figure who was interested in punishing children for bad behavior to a plump, "jolly old elf" with a twinkle in his eye.

But is our gratitude misplaced? Is it possible that Moore didn't actually write "The Night Before Christmas" but (in an act of "Scroogery") stole the credit from another writer? Professor Don Foster certainly thinks so.

The Professor Is In
Foster is an English professor at Vassar College in New York state, but more important, he analyzes works of literature to

compare a questionable text's writing style to an author's established work. The goal? To prove or disprove authorship.

What initially made Foster suspicious about Clement Moore's authoring "A Visit from St. Nicholas" was the fact that Moore didn't claim to have written it until more than 20 years after it was published. The poem first appeared anonymously in the *Troy Sentinel* (a newspaper in Troy, New York) in 1823. But Moore's name didn't come up until 1837, and even then, Moore kept mum about it. It wasn't until 1844 that he quietly included the poem in a collection of his works.

Foster couldn't help wondering why Moore was so reluctant to claim authorship, especially of a poem that had become such a much-loved favorite. So using software that he created himself, Foster went looking for the answer. He came up with a startling conclusion: the real author was a Poughkeepsie native named Henry Beekman Livingston.

The Evidence

Livingston was an American commander during the Revolutionary War and a poet of Dutch-American descent. He often wrote in an anapestic tetrameter—putting the accent on every third syllable and repeating that four times in each line—just like "A Visit from St. Nicholas." More importantly, though, his verse was genial, playful, and clearly written by a man who loved children. Clement Moore, on the other hand, has been described as a dour, colorless fellow. Many of his other poems and writings are marked by a stern approach to parenting: he was irritated by "clamorish girls" and "boisterous boys" and often

scolded them in verse, urging them to resist earthly pleasures and always be aware of their mortality. And "dread" was one of his favorite words: it appeared more times than any other in his writing.

The more Foster looked, the more inconsistencies he found. He discovered that Moore was known for his tirades against tobacco, calling it "opium's treacherous aid." Yet in "A Visit from St. Nicholas," Santa smokes a pipe. And then there's the reindeer issue. When the poem was first printed in 1823, Santa's last two reindeer were called "Dunder" and "Blixem," the Dutch words for thunder and lightning that Livingston, having Dutch ancestry, would likely have used. But when Moore wrote out a copy of the poem late in his life, he spelled the reindeer's names as "Donder and Blitzen," their German variations. That was reasonable since Moore spoke German, but inconsistent with the earlier printed version.

And finally, there's the issue of plagiarism. Literary detective Foster discovered a sheep-farming manual Moore had donated to a New York library. On the inside cover, Moore included an inscription that indicated he'd translated the text personally from the original French. But a copyright note buried in the fine print on the last page lists someone else as the sole translator.

Why Not Take Credit?

Foster also wondered . . . if Moore did write the poem, why did he wait so long to say so? Moore always claimed that he was embarrassed by the fuss over what he called "a mere trifle," saying that it diminished his reputation as a serious scholar and writer. He explained that he only included the poem in his 1844 edition of collected verse because his family asked him to. Yet Foster discovered that before Moore came forward with his claim, he wrote to the publisher of the *Troy Sentinel*, the newspaper that first printed "A Visit from St. Nicholas." In the letter, Moore asked if anyone knew where the poem had come from. He was told that anyone who might have known had died years before.

The Proof's in the Pocketbook?

Livingston died in 1828, only a few years after the poem was published. He was 79, and his advanced age, as well as the fact that most of his verse was written to amuse family and friends, may explain why he never made a case for authorship. No original manuscript of the poem has ever been found. (Moore's handwritten versions, reindeer misspellings and all, date from after 1844.) So, because there's no way to prove that Livingston was the real author, Foster's idea remains just a theory.

The poem's fans, though, remain loyally by its side . . . and, in some cases, by Moore's. Those hand-written copies Moore made late in his life continue to be among the most valuable documents in American history. In 1997 one of them sold for $211,000.

*   *   *

Sir Santa

For 54 years (since he was 14 years old), Edward Joseph Cooper of Belfast, Northern Ireland, has bought toys to distribute to underprivileged kids at Christmas. He does it all on his own and has gone out of his way to downplay any public recognition for his work. But no matter how secret this Santa has wanted to be, one VIP noticed and rewarded his actions. In 2007 Queen Elizabeth II made Edward Joseph Cooper an MBE (Member of the British Empire) for his services to the community in Northern Ireland. (Oh, and besides giving Christmas gifts to thousands of kids, Cooper also donates Easter eggs to orphans.)

Yuletide Yuks Strike Back

One list of bad jokes is never enough!

What do you call a group of chess fanatics bragging about their games in a hotel lobby?
Chess nuts boasting in an open foyer!

What does Santa say when he falls down the chimney backward?
Oh! Oh! Oh!

Who's the better fighter—an elf or a chicken?
An elf—he's no chicken.

Where do you find elves?
Where you left them!

What did one angel say to the other angel?
Halo there!

Bah Humbug!

As great a holiday as it is, Christmas seems to bring out the worst in some people. Here are our nominees for Scrooge of the Year.

Ouch!

A dentist gave his assistant a $30 gift certificate for Christmas, which was great until she discovered that the certificate could be redeemed only at an upscale boutique owned by the dentist's wife . . . and that carried nothing even close to $30.

I Hat You

The Great Dickens Christmas Fair in San Francisco used to give out cash bonuses at Christmas. But in 2006 the fair stopped doing that. Instead, each employee got a white painter's cap with the words "Bah Humbug" printed on it.

Spud

Every year, a consumer electronics company in the English town of Grimsby gives its workers the same Christmas bonus: a sack of potatoes. (The owner's cousin owns a potato farm.)

He Sees You When You're Working

Andy Grove, the former CEO of Intel, became notorious for his "Scrooge Memo," in which he pointedly reminded employees of their obligation to work a full day on Christmas Eve—or else.

And Goodwill to None

Richard Martin, a 71-year-old apartment manager in Bay Ridge, New York, got upset one year when someone tore down the Christmas decorations he'd put up in the lobby of his apartment building. So he wrote the following note and sent it to all his tenants: "Dear sc*mb*g: If I catch you, I will kill you where you are. You don't want to f*** with the Irish."

Alone in a Manger

Colin Wood of Essex, England, hated Christmas so much that, in 2001, he rented a fallout shelter for $600 so he could lock himself away for the holidays. He told the BBC that Christmas provoked too many family arguments and he preferred to avoid the whole thing. (His brother gave him a copy of Dickens's *A Christmas Carol* to read while underground.)

Answers

The Alphabet Carol Quiz, page 23

1. I'm Dreaming of a White Christmas . . . ("White Christmas")

2. Away in a manger, no crib for a bed . . . ("Away in a Manger")

3. Oh, the weather outside is frightful . . . ("Let It Snow! Let It Snow! Let It Snow!")

4. Joy to the world, the Lord is come . . . ("Joy to the World")

5. On the first day of Christmas my true love gave to me . . . ("Twelve Days of Christmas")

6. "I Saw Mommy Kissing Santa Claus"

7. You better watch out, you better not cry . . . ("Santa Claus Is Coming to Town")

8. The first noel the angels did say . . . ("The First Noel")

9. Silent night, holy night . . . ("Silent Night")

10. Frosty the snowman was a jolly happy soul . . . ("Frosty the Snowman")

11. We three kings of Orient are . . . ("We Three Kings")

12. Sleigh bells ring, are you listening? ("Winter Wonderland")

13. It came upon the midnight clear . . . ("It Came Upon the Midnight Clear")

14. Chestnuts roasting on an open fire . . . ("The Christmas Song")

Pop Christmas Quiz, page 137

1. f. John Lennon: "Happy Xmas (War Is Over)"

2. d. Joni Mitchell: "River"

3. j. Ringo Starr: "I Wanna Be Santa Claus"

4. i. Mariah Carey: "All I Want for Christmas is You"

5. c . Madonna: "Santa Baby"

6. g. Paul McCartney: "Wonderful Christmastime"

7. h. Garth Brooks: "Santa Looked a Lot Like Daddy" (Originally sung by Buck Owens.)

8. a. Britney Spears: "My Only Wish (This Year)"

9. b. Bruce Springsteen: "Merry Christmas, Baby"

10. e. Bon Jovi: "I Wish Everyday Could Be Like Christmas"

Bonus Round!

b. Destiny's Child

Party Puzzlers, page 143

1. a. The Bible never mentions the Three Wise Men, only that Magi (members of an ancient Zoroastrian caste of priests in Persia) brought gifts of gold, frankincense, and myrrh.

2. b. In 1223 St. Francis built a manger with an ox and a donkey for the midnight mass in the town of Grecio, Italy.

3. b. "Noel" comes from the French phrase *les bonnes nouvelles*, which means "the good news," or gospel.

4. c. The signal to evacuate was the radio announcement, "The temperature in Saigon is 112 degrees and rising," followed by the playing of Bing Crosby's "White Christmas."

5. c. Twenty-three-year-old Judy Garland sang, "Have Yourself a Merry Little Christmas" in the 1944 film *Meet Me in St. Louis*. The song, however, didn't become a popular Christmas tune until Frank Sinatra recorded it in 1957.

6. c. Working-class Londoners started saving their pennies for the Christmas goose 13 weeks before Christmas by making contributions to the Goose Club run by their local pub. The geese were distributed on Christmas Eve. People who contributed more money got a bottle of gin as well.

7. a. Ward Bond and Frank Faylen played Bert and Ernie opposite Donna Reed and James Stewart in the 1946 Frank Capra classic.

Rewriting the Carols, page 166

1. "Hark! The Herald Angels Sing"

2. "Deck the Halls"

3. "The Little Drummer Boy"

4. "Sleigh Ride"

5. "Silent Night, Holy Night"

6. "Walking in a Winter Wonderland"

7. "Chestnuts Roasting on an Open Fire"

8. "I'll Have a Blue Christmas Without You"

9. "Come, All Ye Faithful"

10. "Frosty the Snowman"

11. "We Three Kings of Orient Are"

12. "Hallelujah Chorus"

13. "I Saw Mommy Kissing Santa Claus"

14. "All I Want for Christmas Is My Two Front Teeth"

15. "The Twelve Days of Christmas

Uncle John's Bathroom Reader: For Holiday Lovers

Find these and other great *Uncle John's Bathroom Reader* titles online at www.bathroomreader.com. Or contact us:

Bathroom Readers' Institute
PO Box 1117
Ashland, OR 97520
888.488.4642

The Last Page

Sit down and be counted!

Become a member of the Bathroom Readers' Institute! No join-up fees, monthly minimums or maximums, organized dance parties, quilting bees, solicitors, annoying phone calls (we only have one phone line), spam—or any other canned meat product—to worry about . . . just the chance to get our fabulous monthly newsletter and (if you want) some extremely cool Uncle John's stuff.

So check out our Web site: www.bathroomreader.com

Or send us a letter:
Uncle John's Bathroom Reader
Portable Press
10350 Barnes Canyon Road
San Diego, CA 92121

Or email us at unclejohn@btol.com.

Hope you enjoyed the book. Merry Christmas! And if you're skipping to the end, go back and finish!